HIS MAJESTY'S LOYAL INTERNEE: FRED UHLMAN IN CAPTIVITY

Frontispiece: Photograph of Fred Uhlman and daughter, 1941.
Courtesy of the estate of Fred Uhlman.

His Majesty's Loyal Internee: Fred Uhlman in Captivity

CHARMIAN BRINSON,
ANNA MÜLLER-HÄRLIN,
JULIA WINCKLER

VALLENTINE MITCHELL
LONDON • CHICAGO

First published in 2009 by Vallentine Mitchell

Catalyst House, 720 Centennial Court
Centennial Park, Elstree
Herts, WD6 3SY, UK

814 N. Franklin Street
Chicago, Illinois
60610, USA

www.vmbooks.com

British Library Cataloguing in Publication Data

Brinson, Charmian
'HM loyal internee' : Fred Uhlman in captivity
1. Uhlman, Fred - Imprisonment 2. Uhlman, Fred - Diaries
3. Prisoners of war - Isle of Man - Biography 4. Refugees,
Jewish - Great Britain - Biography 5. Germans - Great
Britain - Evacuation and relocation, 1940-1945 6. World
War, 1939-1945 - Prisoners and prisons, British
I. Title II. Müller-Härlin, Anna III. Winckler, Julia
IV. Uhlman, Fred
940.5'317'4279'092

Library of Congress Cataloging in Publication Data
has been applied for

ISBN 978 0 85303 930 3 (cloth)
ISBN 978 0 85303 920 4 (paper)

Contents

Illustrations

Book cover:
Prisoners behind barbed wire netting.
Illustration used in *Captivity* (London: Jonathan Cape, 1946). 1941 Pen and black ink and charcoal. 202 mm x 326 mm.
Original at British Museum [BM], PRN: PDB20491. Gift of the artist 1971.
Reproduced by kind permission of the BM.

Frontispiece:
Photograph of Fred Uhlman and daughter Caroline, 1941.
Courtesy of the estate of Fred Uhlman.

Figure 1. Map of Hutchinson Internment Camp, Douglas, Isle of Man.
Manx National Heritage, Maps and Plans DG4L.
Reproduced by kind permission of Manx National Heritage.

Figures 2 and 3. Catalogue 2nd Art Exhibition, 19 November 1940, in Hutchinson Camp.
Departments of Documents Folder [DDF], Imperial War Museum [IWM] 78/19/1.
Reproduced by kind permission of the IWM.

Figure 4. Artists' letter to the *New Statesman and Nation*, 17 August 1940.
Reproduced by kind permission of the *New Statesman*, © 'all rights reserved'.

Figure 5. Lecture Programme no.17, Cultural Department, Hutchinson Camp (11–17 November 1940).

DDF, IWM 78/19/1.
Reproduced by kind permission of the IWM.

Figure 6. 'Art Exhibition', review of the First Art Exhibition in Hutchinson Camp, *The Camp*, no.1, 21 September 1940.
Reproduced by kind permission of the IWM.

Figure 7. 'The Campfather's Address to the Commander on Occasion of the Opening of the Second Art Exhibition', *The Camp*, no.10, 24 November 1940.
Reproduced by kind permission of the IWM.

Figure 8. *Ascot*, 'Internment series', 1940. Illustration used in *Captivity* (London: Jonathan Cape, 1946).
1940. Pen and black ink. 176 mm x 228 mm.
Original at BM, PRN: PDB21863. Gift of the artist, 1958.
Reproduced by kind permission of BM.

Figure 9. *Ascot – Two Figures Reading by the Fence*. 'Internment series', 1940. Ink and conté on paper, 165 mm x 222 mm.
IWM ART LD 7530 Ascot, 1940. Gift of the artist, 11-1979.
Reproduced by kind permission of the IWM.

Figure 10. *Untitled*, view over Hutchinson Square, 1940.
Linocut, 5 x 5 x 4 inches approx.
DDF IWM 78/19/1.
Reproduced by kind permission of the IWM.

Figure 11. *Untitled*. Child in a fantastic landscape, from 'A mon enfant nouveau né' Series, 1940; in foreground corpses and skeletons, beyond gallows and a child seen from behind.
Illustration used in *Captivity* (London: Jonathan Cape, 1946).
Pen, black ink with charcoal, 205 mm x 253 mm.
Original at BM, PRN: PDB20499. Gift of the artist, 1971.
Reproduced by kind permission of the BM.

Figure 12. *Untitled*. Girl with balloon and gallows, 1940.
Linocut, 5 x 5 x 4 inches approx.
DDF IWM 78/19/1.
Reproduced by kind permission of the IWM.

Figure 13. *Untitled.* Child with balloon among ruined buildings, 1940.
Illustration from *Captivity* (London: Jonathan Cape, 1946).
Pen and black ink and charcoal, 178 mm x 230 mm.
Original at BM, PRN: PDB20494. Gift of the artist, 1971.
Reproduced by kind permission of the BM.

Figure 14. *Untitled.* War fantasy with crucified Christ, 1940.
Illustration used in *Captivity* (London: Jonathan Cape, 1946).
Pen, black ink and charcoal. 205 mm x 253 mm.
Original at BM, PRN: PDB20495. Gift of the artist, 1971.
Reproduced by kind permission of the BM.

Figure 15. *Untitled.* Child hanging from a gallows, 1940.
Illustration used in *Captivity* (London: Jonathan Cape, 1946).
Pen, black ink, charcoal, 179 mm x 214 mm.
Original at BM, PRN: PDB20497. Gift of the artist, 1971.
Reproduced by kind permission of the BM.

Figure 16. *Untitled.* Skull, flowers, gallows, 1940.
Linocut, 5 x 5 x 4 inches approx.
DDF IWM 78/19/1.
Reproduced by kind permission of the IWM.

Figure 17. '*Das Totenschiff – The Ship of the Dead*, 'Internment series', 1940.
Ink, wash, pencil and conté on paper. 247 mm x 228 mm.
IWM ART LD 7525. Gift of the artist, 11-1979.
Reproduced by kind permission of the IWM.

Figure 18. *Untitled.* Boat and rowers, 1940. Linocut.
5 x 5 x 4 inches approx.
DDF: IWM 78/19/1.
Reproduced by kind permission of the IWM.

Figure 19. *Untitled.* Dance of Death, 1940.
Illustration used in *Captivity* (London: Jonathan Cape, 1946).
Pen, black ink with charcoal. 195 mm x 167 mm.
Original at BM PRN: PDB20450. Gift of the artist, 1971.
Reproduced by kind permission of the BM.

Figure 20. *Little Girl with War Criminals*, 1940.
Illustration used in *Captivity* (London: Jonathan Cape, 1946).
Location of original unknown.
Reproduced by kind permission of the Uhlman estate.

Figure 21. *Untitled*. From 'Ecclesia Militans' series. Four monks in flight, 1940.
Illustration used in *Captivity* (London: Jonathan Cape, 1946).
Pen, black ink, with grey wash, charcoal and graphite. 215 mm x 29 mm.
Original at BM, PRN: PDB20501. Gift of the artist, 1971.
Reproduced by kind permission of the BM.

Figure 22. *Clothing Caught on a Branch and Lying in a Field*, 'Internment series', 1940.
Ink, wash, pencil and conté on paper.
190 mm x 260 mm.
IWM ART LD 7522. Gift of the artist, 11-1979.
Reproduced by kind permission of the IWM.

Figure 23. Uhlman poem and untitled linocut of skull and gallows, 1940.
5 x 5 x 4 inches approx.
DDF: IWM 78/19/1.
Reproduced by kind permission of the IWM.

Acknowledgements

First and foremost, we are indebted to Caroline Compton and to Manx National Heritage for their generous support of this project. We also owe grateful thanks to Caroline Compton and Francis Uhlman for kindly permitting us to reproduce some of their late father's previously unpublished writings as well as his internment art works. In addition, we should like to express our thanks to the Imperial War Museum (in particular Pauline Allwright, Dil Banerjee, Elizabeth Bowers, Michael Moody and Roderick Suddaby) and the British Museum (in particular Jennifer Ramkalawon and Axelle Russo) for permission to reproduce Fred Uhlman's art works from their collections; to the *New Statesman* for permission to reproduce the artists' letter of 17 August 1940; to the Churchill Archives Centre, Cambridge, and once again to Manx National Heritage and the Imperial War Museum for permitting us access to archive materials; and to Peter Daniel who shared with us papers and mementos belonging to his late father, Major H.O. Daniel, Commander of Hutchinson Camp. Finally we should like to thank the following for their kind interest and assistance: Marietta Bearman, Yvonne Cresswell, Stefan Feuchtwang, Alan Franklin, Anna Nyburg, Rosemary Poole, Anke Winckler, Lutz Winckler and Erna Woodgate.

Foreword

Caroline Compton

My father's internment at Ascot and then on the Isle of Man was a subject often referred to during his lifetime. Surreal, unjust, sometimes humorous. He often mentioned the 'university campus' and used to recite poetry by the artist Kurt Schwitters; Schwitters' portrait of him, undertaken at Hutchinson Camp, was hidden away in the attic studio of our family house in Hampstead but it was there all the same. Now I can see it reproduced on a postcard. (The original painting now hangs in the Hatton Gallery, Newcastle upon Tyne.) Some of my father's drawings undertaken in the internment camps are dedicated to 'mon enfant nouveau né' and are a further reminder.

Spending years of his life as a lawyer in Stuttgart defending anti-Nazis was, in my father's eyes, a good qualification for his antifascist credentials. His involvement with the Social Democratic Party led to his working with Kurt Schumacher who, following years of imprisonment in concentration camps, would become leader of the SPD in West Germany after the war. My father's internment in England, he felt, was unfair but he could also see, with hindsight, how the British government was driven to react to thousands of Germans and Austrians living in this country when we were at war. He always maintained that if he had known how long his sentence was to last, it would have been more bearable. He was only behind barbed wire for six months but it could have been for years. The worst punishment for internees was a form of torture known as 'release'. Every week, a few of them were allowed to leave.

At a time when abstract art in this country was still suspect, my father had a short but successful career as a 'New Romantic', exhibiting in mixed and one-man shows in galleries in London. (During the 1940s and into the early 1970s, London only had about thirty galleries showing contemporary art.) When he had a detached retina in one eye in 1969 his painting career came to an end but his writing career took off.

It is more than sixty years since my father's book of drawings of his time in Ascot and the Isle of Man was published. I have always felt that the drawings deserved to be seen again and by a wider public. I am therefore very grateful to the authors of this volume for all the work they have put into this project.

Caroline Compton

Foreword

Yvonne Cresswell

In terms of twentieth-century British history, civilian internment has frequently been considered as a lost footnote amongst the chapters of two World Wars. The subject of civilian internment during the Second World War has slowly become more widely recognized and is now increasingly an object of academic consideration and analysis. It is still, though, a topic that tends to be the subject of a broadbrush approach with few, if any, detailed case studies. Research over recent years has concentrated on the political context of internment and looked at broad themes and topics within the internment experience such as art, culture and living conditions within the various internment camps. This work has been important in providing secure foundations and a wider context for future research, but the time is now ripe for more detailed and specific studies of internment and of the more notable individuals who were part of that experience.

This series of essays and documents, studying and reflecting in depth on the work and internment experience of the artist, Fred Uhlman, is an important contribution to the subject matter. It provides an exemplar for future research on ex-internees, in particular for artists and their lives and work, by illustrating the benefit of concentrating on a single internee and highlighting his own individual and unique experiences. A review of only a few oral history testimonies will indicate that, although many aspects of internment were common to all, each individual tended to perceive the shared internment experiences in his or her own distinct and personal manner, often resulting in widely differing and apparently conflicting testimonies. The objective, factual reality of internment presented in many studies becomes a much more subjective series of individual experiences, ranging from the extremely positive to the very negative, as one moves from the broad canvas to a single brush stroke.

As illustrated in these essays and documents, Uhlman's own perception and record of his internment experiences changed dramatically between the original German Diary written in Hutchinson Camp in 1940 and the much more considered (and revised) English Memoir dating from 1979. A comparison of the two reveals to what extent the individual's perceptions change and develop over time. The attitudes and opinions recorded at the time, which may appear quite raw in retrospect, change gradually through a combination of hindsight and later knowledge which together set the earlier experiences into a broader context.

Another important aspect of this study of Fred Uhlman is the fact that Uhlman is neither confined to nor defined purely by his internment experiences (a potential pitfall when analysing an interned artist). Instead, Uhlman's internment experiences have been positioned within the context of his personal and artistic life in the 1930s and 1940s. As a result, it is possible to consider how his life immediately before internment both informed and affected his internment experience and how that, in turn, influenced the years immediately following his internment.

It is important to bear in mind that, however significant the influence of internment was on an individual's life, it represented no more than one influence. For most people, internment lasted for a period of a few months, and rarely for more than two years out of a whole lifetime. Therefore for Uhlman, as for many ex-internees, internment represented a chapter in his life but not the whole story. *His Majesty's Loyal Internee: Fred Uhlman in Captivity* provides us with glimpses of Uhlman's life before, during and after internment as well as illuminating the broader picture of the internment experience.

Yvonne M. Cresswell
Curator of Social History
Manx National Heritage

PART I

1. *Introduction*

Charmian Brinson, Anna Müller-Härlin, Julia Winckler

PREAMBLE

Firstly to retrace the genesis of this book: in 2001, while carrying out some research at the Imperial War Museum, Julia Winckler, an artist and lecturer at the University of Brighton working mainly in photography, came across a folder containing documents relating to the wartime internment in Britain of the German lawyer, artist and writer, Fred Uhlman. These documents were Uhlman's internment diary, dating from 1940, and his 1979 internment memoir in which he revisited and recast the events of forty years before. The file also contained correspondence between Uhlman, in internment, and his British-born wife and father-in law as well as some original and unpublished linocuts, produced in the internment camp. She approached Charmian Brinson, Professor of German at Imperial College London and a founder member of the Research Centre for German and Austrian Exile Studies (University of London), who recognized the significance of the documents; and Brinson in turn contacted Anna Müller-Härlin, an art historian and expert on the subject of Fred Uhlman's life and work, who had already seen these documents in the Uhlman estate. Between them they agreed to contribute to a book which would make these previously unpublished materials accessible to the general public.

As it happened, the three authors, though each from a different background and discipline, were between them well qualified to produce such a volume. Julia Winckler, who had grown up with stories from internment told to her by her great-aunt and by other family friends, all ex-internees, had earlier pursued a photographic project to explore what residues of camp life (both material and immaterial, i.e. in the form of oral history) there remained on the Isle of Man. During several photographic research visits to the island, Winckler met local residents who remembered the internees (or 'aliens', as they referred to them) back in 1940. In Hutchinson Square, Douglas, she stayed in one of the boarding houses that had previously made up Hutchinson Camp, where the landlady showed her some wooden artefacts she still had in her possession, made by internees. At the edge of the square, she even found a remnant of the old camp railing to be still in place. Indeed, Hutchinson Square has remained virtually unchanged since the 1940s; and, standing in the centre, Winckler found herself strongly reminded of Fred Uhlman's description of it from some sixty years before: 'Imagine a square in the middle of London consisting of some forty small and cheap boarding houses. Surround it with barbed wire and fill each house with between 30 and 40 men of all ages and professions. Imagine all windows painted blue and all electric light bulbs red [...] and you have some notion of the Hutchinson Square Camp in Douglas.'[1]

Charmian Brinson, who has published widely on the subject of German-speaking exile in Britain, originally met Winckler in connection with the latter's internment exhibition in Douglas in 2004. Brinson also has a particular research interest in the wartime internment of aliens and has written and lectured on life in the Rushen women's internment camp at Port Erin and Port St Mary, Isle of Man. In the course of her work, she has interviewed numerous ex-internees, both male and female, as well as local people on the island in order to record their experiences. For the present project, Brinson was fortunate to meet Peter Daniel, the son of the late Commander of Hutchinson Camp, who still has in his possession the album of internee art his father collected, including two pen and ink drawings by Fred Uhlman.

Anna Müller-Härlin, while still a student of art history, had lived in Hampstead where she became interested in the fate of the many émigrés who had found themselves in North London in the 1930s and 1940s. She noticed that, although Fred Uhlman's name was almost invariably mentioned in secondary literature on exile in Britain, his life and work had never been examined in its own right. Müller-Härlin became intrigued as to who the man had been whose former home in Downshire Hill she passed so often: a house which had not only accommodated both the wartime refugee organization the Free German League of Culture and the Artists' Refugee Committee for a time but had also offered hospitality to numerous otherwise homeless refugees. It was through Patience Gray, mainly known as the writer of cookery books, who had known Uhlman, that she came into contact with Uhlman's children Caroline Compton and Francis Uhlman, leading to a warm relationship with them and with émigré friends of their father as well as to her doctorate on Fred Uhlman at the Courtauld Institute of Art.

The present book, *His Majesty's Loyal Internee: Fred Uhlman in Captivity*, which in essence offers multiple interpretations of the same internment experience, can be broken down into three parts: the first consists of introductory material aiming to set the volume as a whole in context; the second reproduces Uhlman's original documents; while the third comments upon these documents and Uhlman's internment images first from a literary, then from an artistic perspective. Thus the first section, which opens with the present chapter, aims to elucidate the origins, structure and aims of this volume as well as to map out Fred Uhlman's life and artistic development, both prior to his seminal internment experience and as an interned artist. This section also offers a historical overview of German-speaking exile in Britain from 1933 onwards, of the British wartime internment policy and, above all, of daily life and conditions in Hutchinson Camp, Douglas, Isle of Man. In addition, in 'Fred Uhlman and the Croft Connection', light is shed on Uhlman's unexpected links, through his marriage, with the British aristocracy, and thus on some of the issues that feature large in the 'Letters from Internment', reproduced in the following section.

The second section, relating closely to the first, consists of the authentic textual material, starting with Uhlman's two internment accounts. The 1940 diary, 'HM Loyal Internee', which was written in German, has been transcribed as fully as possible from the original manuscript (the illegibility of certain words and phrases testify to the conditions under which it was produced). It appears here in the English translation of the authors (and is referred to hereafter as the Internment Diary). The 1979 memoir, entitled 'The Story of *Captivity*', appears in the rather idiosyncratic English in which Uhlman himself wrote it (and is referred to as the Internment Memoir). There follow a number of letters exchanged between Uhlman, in Hutchinson Camp, and his wife Diana, which amply illustrate the tensions of the time and of the specific situation, as well as others to and from Uhlman's father-in-law, Lord Croft, with whom Uhlman 'enjoyed' a strained relationship.

The third section, again intimately linked to the previous two, sets out to interpret and elucidate Uhlman's literary and artistic production in internment. It includes a selection of Uhlman's artwork in internment: four linocuts located at the Imperial War Museum are reproduced here, as are twelve drawings, of which four are similarly from the Imperial War Museum and eight from *Captivity*, the slim volume of drawings Uhlman went on to publish in 1946. Focusing on his literary output, Brinson and Müller-Härlin examine and compare Uhlman's two similar yet divergent internment accounts, the diary and the memoir, as well as a third version of these same events found in his autobiography, *The Making of an Englishman* (1960). In the following chapter, Winckler offers an artist's response to Uhlman's artistic output, relating the latter closely to the singular environment from which it stemmed.

The volume concludes with an epilogue in which Müller-Härlin assesses the impact of exile and internment on Uhlman's later life and work; and, as a guide to further reading, with a select bibliography of literature on the British internment of aliens in the Second World War. With this volume, the three authors hope to contribute to a better understanding of what internment signified for an artist and for artistic production. They also wish to bring Uhlman's unique – though largely forgotten – internment drawings and linocuts, on the one hand, and his internment writings on the other to the attention of a wider public.

FRED UHLMAN'S UNUSUAL CAREER

The German-Jewish lawyer, painter and writer Fred (Manfred) Uhlman (1901–85) was born in Stuttgart.[2] His father was a well-off cotton merchant. Uhlman had a younger sister and the family lived a comfortable middle-class life; however the inability of his parents to show affection turned Uhlman's childhood into an unhappy one. He received a secular upbringing[3] and attended the renowned Eberhard-Ludwigs-Gymnasium in Stuttgart where, in 1920, he took his Abitur. He studied law in Freiburg, Munich and Tübingen and worked as a lawyer in Stuttgart from 1927 to 1933. As an active member of the Social Democratic Party, he was forced to flee from his home country in March 1933 in order to escape arrest after Hitler had gained power in January. Until March 1936, Uhlman lived in Paris where, as a refugee, he was no longer able to practise his profession as a lawyer. According to Uhlman, it was his cousin, the Paris-based painter Paul Elsas, who encouraged him to paint professionally from 1934 onwards. Uhlman had painted in his spare time back in Stuttgart, but he had never had any formal art training. Through Elsas, he began to mix in artistic circles. He used to frequent the famous Café du Dôme where he met and became a friend of the German art critic Paul Westheim (1886–1963), former editor of the art review *Das Kunstblatt* in Berlin. Westheim viewed Uhlman's paintings and began to support him. Following his debut as an artist in group exhibitions from 1935 onwards, Uhlman began to be praised as a 'naïve' artist. He had his first one-man show in Paris in February 1936, a few weeks before he left Paris for Spain. Although he settled in London that same year, he continued to have solo exhibitions in Paris until 1939.[4] Admittedly Uhlman could not live from his painting activity and was dependent on his savings. However, for an émigré painter, as unknown in his home country as he was in France, he received an unusual amount of attention not only from German exile periodicals such as the *Pariser Tageblatt* (later *Pariser Tageszeitung*), but also in the French press. In 1938, the Musée du Jeu de Paume, the Musée de Grenoble as well as the Ministère de l'Education all acquired works by Uhlman.

Characteristic of Uhlman's early works in which he primarily pictured Parisian city scenes was their small canvas size. Uhlman was indeed 'naïve' in the sense that he lacked an understanding of contemporary modern art. At that early stage of his career, he was also entirely untutored in terms of technique and paid no attention to perspective.[5] However, Uhlman was aware of his technical shortcomings and was able to exploit them as a virtue in his works. Moreover, he worked on his technique, with the result that over the decades his style of painting did undergo some change.

From April to July 1936, Uhlman stayed in the Spanish fishing village Tossa del Mar with the painter Oskar Zügel, an acquaintance of his from Stuttgart, until the outbreak of the Spanish Civil War. It was in Tossa del Mar that in April he met the young Englishwoman Diana Croft (1912–99) who was travelling through Spain together with her friend Betty Sackville-West. In September of the same year, Uhlman arrived in London; by November Fred and Diana were married. It was at the Uhlmans' home, 47 Downshire Hill in Hampstead, that in the autumn of 1938 the Free German League of Culture was founded, with Uhlman as one of its co-founders. The

Artists' Refugee Committee also operated from the Uhlmans' home, the Uhlmans being amongst the Committee's instigators and Diana one of the Committee's major figures.[6]

That the Uhlmans fell in love with one another and subsequently married constituted an act of rebellion, at least on Diana's part. Diana came from a distinguished upper-class family; her father was the well-known ultra-Conservative politician, Brigadier-General Sir Henry Page Croft (later Lord Croft) (1881–1947). Croft was notorious for his nationalism and his devotion to the defence of the British Empire. He strongly disapproved of his daughter's decision to marry a penniless German-Jewish painter. The political gulf between Lord Croft and the Uhlmans also has to be considered within the wider context of the ideological clashes of the time. Lord Croft was fighting for a world order which was in decline by the 1930s: one which involved holding on to the British Empire and sustaining it by any possible means. The Uhlmans, on the other hand, although far from being radicals, were determined socialists who fought against fascism. Their different political standpoints, which reached a peak during Uhlman's internment in 1940, will be looked at in 'Fred Uhlman and the Croft Connection', below.

In 1938, Uhlman had his first London solo show at the renowned Zwemmer Gallery.[7] By this time, his paintings had changed dramatically in mood: he had moved to focusing on motifs such as deserted chateaux and cemeteries and to using a much more opaque palette. His paintings had begun to express a deep melancholy often achieved either by a complete lack of human presence or by a sole figure, seen from the back, wandering in the scenery of the painting. The Zwemmer exhibition marked the beginning of his career in England. Many critics commented on his work approvingly as being 'romantic' and 'melancholic'. In 1939, he was included in the 'Living Art in England' exhibition, organized by the London Gallery.[8] This was one of the last important British avant-garde exhibitions before the outbreak of the war, focusing mainly on Surrealist and Constructivist art. Uhlman's inclusion in this context was thus an exception and testifies to a growing interest in his art; in the catalogue his work was labelled 'independent'.[9] However, the following year brought an unexpected temporary interruption to his promising start in the London art world.

THE INTERNED ARTIST

In June 1940, like a large number of German-speaking refugees, Uhlman was interned. Despite having been categorized as a 'C' class 'enemy alien' (see following chapter), Uhlman was arrested on 25 June in Wareside near Ware. He was visiting his wife Diana, who was staying there with her aunt while expecting her first child. After approximately three and a half weeks at Ascot, Uhlman was interned in Hutchinson Camp on the Isle of Man from mid-July until 31 December 1940. The internment of enemy aliens in Britain in 1940 is examined in Chapter Two below, as is the busy intellectual life in Hutchinson Camp, which offered a considerable amount of distraction for the internees.

All the internment camps included artists among their inmates, but a particularly large number of them were held at Hutchinson. Many of the artists had previously met in London under the aegis of the Free German League of Culture (FGLC), the Artists' Refugee Committee (ARC) and the Artists' International Association (AIA). The sculptor Paul Hamann, for example, with whom Uhlman had led the FGLC's artists' section until their arrest, was interned at Hutchinson, as were the sculptors Siegfried Charoux and Georg Ehrlich, who had both exhibited at the FGLC's first group exhibition at the Wertheim Gallery in 1939.

During the six months of his internment, Uhlman produced well over one hundred and fifty drawings in charcoal and in black and brown ink. In the post-war years, Uhlman donated the majority of these drawings to museums in both England and Germany.[10] Because of the shortage of artists' materials in the camp, sketchbooks, pens and pencils became key tools.[11] Various organizations such as the ARC and the AIA sent materials to the camps which slightly improved matters. However, Uhlman continued drawing even when oil paints became available.[12] He seems to have only made three oil paintings at Hutchinson, all of which were exhibited in the Second Art Exhibition in November.[13]

Uhlman worked, on average, on one drawing a day. This is evident from the Internment Diary, in which he meticulously traced his productivity. On some days he was too depressed to work though on others made two or more drawings. Uhlman also learned to make linocuts,[14] a technique with which he was previously unfamiliar, and also began to work on sculpture.[15]

The work he produced in internment can be defined as an artistic period distinct from his work, both before and after.[16] The drawings are not only formally different from his previous œuvre, but are also distinctive in terms of content. Unusually for Uhlman, the human figure is the main focus. He invented a symbol, a girl with a balloon, to stand for hope of a better future in a world dominated by war and destruction. While various stylistic details in the drawings, such as black flying birds or dead trees, appear in his paintings before and after internment, neither the girl and the balloon, nor the representation of priests who also feature in many of the drawings, was taken up again. The drawings must be seen as a direct product of Uhlman's experience of internment. In 'Should the artist portray his age?': Reflections on Fred Uhlman's Internment Art Works', below, Uhlman's drawings – more specifically the selection of drawings which Uhlman donated to the Imperial War Museum in London – are considered as a means of witnessing and expressing this period.

In 1946, a selection of twenty-four drawings was published by Jonathan Cape. The writer and critic, Raymond Mortimer (1895–1980)[17] wrote the introduction for the slim hardback, entitled *Captivity*. Mortimer summarized the force of the works as follows: 'The uncertainty, the frustration and the indefinable anguish of captivity are reflected in the drawings made by Fred Uhlman, as he brooded over the fate of the world from which he was isolated.'[18] The drawings impressively capture a historical period dominated by anxiety and terror. Uhlman's drawings operate within conventional representational means, yet at the same time he brilliantly succeeded in conveying uncanny visions of a destroyed world, in making critical statements about the Church, and in expressing hope for a better future through the figure of the little girl.

On 1 January 1941, Uhlman joined Diana and their daughter Caroline in Bambers Green, near Great Bardfield. The Uhlmans had purchased a small cottage there in order to escape the London bombings, and Diana had moved to Bambers Green from Wareside with their first child. In 1943, their son Francis was also born there. The family returned to 47 Downshire Hill in London in 1944.[19] In January 1942, a selection of Uhlman's internment drawings was exhibited at the Free German League of Culture in Upper Park Road, Hampstead.[20] This was the last time that Uhlman had the possibility of showing the drawings in public. In the museums to which

Uhlman donated the drawings, they have been carefully stored away – and forgotten. However, the drawings are a powerful witness to the depression Uhlman experienced during his internment, while at the same time he never gave up hope of a better future for mankind.

NOTES

1. Fred Uhlman as cited by Raymond Mortimer, in introduction to *Captivity: Twenty-four drawings by Fred Uhlman* (London: Jonathan Cape, 1946), p.1.
2. On Fred Uhlman see Anna Müller-Härlin (Plodeck), 'The Making of Fred Uhlman: Life and Work of the Painter and Writer in Exile' Unpublished doctoral thesis, Courtauld Institute of Art, London, 2004.
3. His father was an agnostic and Uhlman received no religious Jewish education at home. Like so many secularized Jewish families at the time, they celebrated Christmas.
4. 'Exposition Fred Uhlman', Le Niveau, Paris, 6–16 February 1936; 'Exposition Fred Uhlman', Le Niveau, Paris, 16–30 January 1937; 'Fred Uhlman Œuvres Récentes', Le Niveau, Paris, 7–21 March 1938; 'Fred Uhlman Œuvres Récentes', Jeanne Castel, Paris, 1–15 July 1939.
5. See, for example, *Das Restaurant*, ca. 1934, oil on board, 26 x 33.5 cm, in the possession of Caroline Compton, London.
6. On the Uhlmans and their involvement with the FGLC and the ARC, see Anna Müller-Härlin, '"It all happened in this street, 47 Downshire Hill": Fred Uhlman and the Free German League of Culture', in Shulamith Behr and Marian Malet (eds), *Arts in Exile in Britain 1933–1945: Politics and Cultural Identity: The Yearbook of the Research Centre for German and Austrian Exile Studies*, VI (Amsterdam: Rodopi, 2004 [2005]), pp.241–5.
7. 'Fred Uhlman', Zwemmer Gallery, London, 6 July–6 August 1938.
8. 'Living Art in England', 18 January–11 February 1939, London Gallery, London. In 1939, Uhlman also participated in the 'FDKB Group Exhibition of German, Austrian and Czechoslovakian Painters and Sculptors', 29 June–3 July 1939, Wertheim Gallery, London and 'Cities and Suburbs. Stephen Bone, Horst Nessler, Fred Uhlman', 29 June–21 July 1939, Arcade Gallery, London.
9. Further émigré participants were John Heartfield, Oskar Kokoschka, Naum Gabo and Piet Mondrian.
10. British Museum, London (29 works); Imperial War Museum, London (25); Fitzwilliam Museum, Cambridge (32); Staatsgalerie der Stadt Stuttgart (38); Galerie der Stadt Stuttgart (today Kunstmuseum Stuttgart) (23).
11. The artists became extremely inventive. See Klaus Hinrichsen, 'Visual Arts behind the Wire', in David Cesarani and Tony Kushner (eds), *The Internment of Aliens in Twentieth-Century Britain* (London: Frank Cass, 1993), pp.191 ff.
12. Uhlman diary entry, 30 September 1940: 'Painting doesn't appeal to me at the moment. Pictures are inexpressive, without experience and freedom. Just want to draw' (see Uhlman, Internment Diary, reproduced in this volume). Uhlman possibly gave these notes their title at a later date.
13. 'Second Art Exhibition 19 November 1940 in Hutchinson Camp'.
14. Weissenborn discovered a laundry mangle which he used for making prints. See Hinrichsen, 'Visual Arts', p. 193: 'The great number of prints produced in Hutchinson Camp have probably gone through this mangle.'
15. Uhlman, Internment Diary, 18 and 21 November 1940. A caricature by Erich Kahn exists in which he portrayed Klaus Hinrichsen attempting to sculpt, while Fred Uhlman, gripping his own sculpture, looks aghast. Letter from Klaus Hinrichsen to Anna Müller-Härlin, 23 July 2003.
16. On Uhlman's internment drawings see Anna Müller-Härlin, 'Fred Uhlman's Internment Drawings', in Behr and Malet (eds), *Arts in Exile*, pp.135–63.
17. Raymond Mortimer was a friend of the Uhlmans. He supported Uhlman's career in the

later 1930s and the 1940s. In 1943, he became godfather to their son, Francis.
18. Raymond Mortimer, 'Introduction', in *Captivity: Twenty-four drawings by Fred Uhlman* (London: Jonathan Cape, 1946), p.1.
19. Fred Uhlman, *The Making of an Englishman* (London: Gollancz, 1960), p. 248. However, Uhlman's daughter Caroline Compton believes her parents returned to London a year earlier, in 1943 (letter to Anna Müller-Härlin, 24 September 2006).
20. 'Zeichnungen, entstanden auf der Isle of Man, Ölbilder (Erinnerungen an Frankreich)', Free German League of Culture, London, 15–31 January 1942.

2. *Exile, Internment – and a Camp 'full of once and future Very Important Persons'*

Charmian Brinson

There were, in September 1939, upwards of 70,000 German-speaking refugees in Britain, principally from Germany, Austria and Czechoslovakia, who had been compelled to flee their country on racial and/or political grounds. Hitler's rise to power in Germany in 1933 and subsequent events such as the promulgation of the Nuremberg Laws in 1935, the German annexation of Austria in March 1938 and the 'Crystal Night' pogrom of November 1938 had each given rise to successive waves of emigration. After the outbreak of war in September 1939, these refugees in Britain were deemed 'enemy aliens', regardless of the anti-Nazi record that a number of them, like Fred Uhlman, could boast, or the persecution at the hands of the Nazis that many of them had endured.

As part of the British wartime security measures, around 25,000 German-speaking men and 4,000 women – more exact figures are hard to establish – were arrested and interned for a longer or shorter period during the Second World War, though for the vast majority of them none of this would happen before mid-1940.[1] For a small minority, however, the process was set in train even before the outbreak of war when 415 people on the MI5 'Security List' were arrested and imprisoned.[2] Soon after, all German and Austrian nationals were required to appear in front of one of the Alien Tribunals set up throughout the country to be graded according to their degree of perceived security risk, with 'A' indicating a risk to British security, 'B' that some doubt could be held to exist and 'C' that loyalty to the British cause was not in doubt. While the majority of genuine refugees from National Socialism did indeed receive the correct 'C' categorization, the confusion pervading the whole system was such that mistakes and inconsistencies occurred that took months or even years to rectify.

Following categorization, 569 category 'A' aliens,[3] i.e. those deemed a high security risk, were also arrested and held either in prison or in one of the makeshift interim internment camps that were set up initially in former holiday camps, racecourses and the like. However, for the most part the 'B' and 'C' aliens were left, though subject to certain restrictions, to continue their normal lives during the months of the 'phoney war'. This period came to an end, though, in May and June 1940, when the war took a decided turn for the worse as German troops invaded and occupied one country after another: Denmark, Norway, Holland, Belgium and finally France. With the invasion of Britain apparently imminent, large sections of the British public and press started to demand the internment of all enemy aliens to guard against possible 'Fifth Column' activity, such as had been reported in the occupied countries. Sir Nevile Bland, for instance, British Ambassador to The Hague at the time Holland was invaded, compiled a report entitled 'Fifth Column Menace' that recommended: '*All* Germans and Austrians, at least, ought to be interned at once.'[4] His report, which purported to draw on his own recent experience, had considerable influence in British official circles. The *Daily Mail*, which throughout the 1930s had been sympathetic to the rise of fascism, and other likeminded newspapers now began to conduct a campaign against the refugees, with G. Ward Price, for one, maintaining in his article of 24 May 1940 that:

> All refugees from Austria, Germany and Czechoslovakia, men and women alike, should be drafted without delay to a remote part of the country and kept under strict supervision [...] As the head of a Balkan State said to me last month: 'In Britain you fail to realize that *every* German is an agent.'[5]

Although a policy of mass alien internment had indeed been carried out during the First World War, a similar policy had not been the initial intention of the British authorities this time round, not least because of the refugee status of the large majority of German speakers in Britain. Such was the prevailing mood of panic in the country, however, that the Home Office bowed to the pressure: category 'B' men were arrested on 16 May 1940, category 'B' women on 27 May, Italians from 10 June and, from 22 June, the category 'C' men, such as Uhlman, who constituted the great majority. Internment camps were established throughout Britain, some of them designed merely as temporary transit camps such as the one at Ascot, to which Uhlman was originally assigned: it was situated in the winter quarters of Bertram Mills' Circus. Following the precedent established in the First World War, more permanent camps were established on the Isle of Man, however, whose insular position offered the authorities a high degree of security. At the same time, considerable numbers of male internees were deported to camps in Canada and Australia – most notoriously on the ill-fated Arandora Star which, carrying both prisoners of war and civilian internees, left Liverpool on 1 July 1940, was torpedoed and then sank with much loss of life.

It was this, as much as anything, that brought about a significant change in public opinion on the question of alien internment. The sight of British officialdom turning on a vulnerable group of men and women gave rise to strong criticism in those sections of the press, like the *Manchester Guardian*, that had consistently supported the refugees. Well known public figures like E.M. Forster and Ralph Vaughan Williams penned letters to *The Times*;[6] similarly, H.G. Wells lodged a protest in *Reynolds News* under the heading 'J'accuse'.[7] In a powerful article in the *Evening Standard*, the young Michael Foot posed the question, 'Why not lock up General de Gaulle?' before making the case for 'all who can give proof of their solid anti-Nazi and anti-Fascist resolution' to be welcomed as allies.[8]

At the same time, in Parliament, several lengthy debates took place on the subject of internment, among them the celebrated six-hour Commons debate of 10 July 1940. Major Victor Cazalet, Eleanor Rathbone, Colonel Josiah Wedgwood, George Strauss, Wilfrid Roberts, Sidney Silverman, Reginald Sorensen and Philip Noel-Baker, all well known advocates for the refugees, were among those who spoke out passionately on this occasion.[9] In the Lords, the Bishop of Chichester was one of those to draw attention

> to the strangeness of the decision taken by the Government under great pressure which has had the effect of placing men

> and women, who have been rescued from Hitlerism and who are full of gratitude to this country, in internment camps in this country because the British authorities, and some portion of the British public, suppose these persons are anxious to bring the Nazis who are their bitterest enemies here into England.[10]

Largely in response to this considerable public and parliamentary pressure, three White Papers were issued, the first, on 31 July 1940, bearing the title *German and Austrian Civilian Internees: Categories of Persons Eligible for Release from Internment and Procedure to be Followed in Applying for Release*. Eighteen different categories were listed here. They included those, like the old and the young, the invalid and infirm, who clearly should have been exempted from internment in the first place, together with the internees of greatest use to the war effort: key workers in industry or persons engaged in agriculture or forestry; those accepted into the Pioneer Corps; doctors and dentists; or scientists, research workers and other persons of academic distinction engaged in work of national importance.[11] This White Paper was widely criticized, however, for being informed by a cynical utilitarianism: there was a clear anomaly in the fact that refugees who had been interned on the basis of security were now being released on the grounds of their usefulness. The eighteen categories for release failed to include, most strikingly, the political exiles – proven anti-Nazis – who had no option but to remain in internment until the second White Paper was issued at the end of August, including in a nineteenth category any person who 'by his writings or speeches or political or official activities [...] has consistently, over a period of years, taken a public and prominent part in opposition to the Nazi system and is actively friendly towards the Allied Cause'.[12]

Fred Uhlman, many of whose Internment Diary entries are concerned with the all-important subject of release, could not claim to belong to any of the nineteen categories and thus had no basis on which to apply for release. Only the third White Paper, published in October 1940 with additional categories that included 'persons of eminent distinction who have made outstanding contributions to Art, Science, Learning or Letters',[13] offered him possible grounds for an application, though the questions he puts to himself in his Internment Memoir (based on Diary entry of 21 October 1940) – 'Am I "eminent" enough? Eminent at all?' – reveal his own grave doubts on the subject of his eligibility. For an application to be successful, prominent individuals and/or institutions were required who were prepared to support an applicant's case. For the interned scientists, for instance, this support was provided by the Royal Society on the advice of such refugee aid bodies as the Society for the Protection of Science and Learning that were well acquainted with the individuals concerned, and could vouch both for their professional standing and for their loyalty. In the case of the interned artists, as we learn from Diana Uhlman's letter to her husband of 29 October 1940, the Royal Academy would support those on whom the Artists' Refugee Committee could submit favourable reports.

Indiscriminate internment appears to have been halted around 15 July 1940, even though no official announcement of this was ever made,[14] with the result that some refugees managed to evade the internment process altogether. The classicist Paul Jacobsthal has recalled the increase in tension in Hutchinson from around this time as, with the general improvement in communications to and from the camp, internees learned that other refugees, no different from themselves, had remained at liberty.[15] As for releases, these proceeded slowly, especially initially, which provided another source of tension in the camp, as did the apparent randomness of the process: the elephant keeper released almost immediately for the sake of his animals, to whom Uhlman and others refer, offers a striking example.[16]

Indeed, after the first White Paper, release became the chief topic of conversation among the internees, while the bombarding of prominent Englishmen and women with letters eliciting support for release applications turned into an all-consuming activity. And gradually the pace at which releases were authorized picked up, with around 450 per week being granted during October 1940 and only slightly fewer in the three months thereafter.[17] A Home Office answer to a Parliamentary Question of Eleanor Rathbone's, on 13 February 1941, revealed that by 8 February 9,081 German and Austrian males – including, of course, Fred Uhlman – and 1,031 females, had had their release authorized;[18] and by mid-1941 most, though certainly not all, of those internees who were indubitably refugees from Nazi oppression and loyal to the British cause had been released from the alien internment camps.

* * * * *

Uhlman's confinement in the interim transit camp at Ascot lasted for just over three weeks. Very little of the Internment Diary from this period remains, though enough to indicate the absolutely basic nature of the 'accommodation' that the circus quarters could offer its 400 inmates, and the dismal food. Other camps in use during the early period included one consisting of rows of tents at Prees Heath, another of an unfinished council estate at Huyton and – worst of all – the vermin-infested Warth Mills, near Bury, in which 2,000 men were held in the most appalling conditions.

For Uhlman at Ascot, the greatest deprivation was that of mail, the total lack of communication with the outside world, which hit him, as an expectant father, particularly hard. By the time he arrived in Hutchinson Camp on the Isle of Man, there would already have been some noticeable improvement in this area (though internee mail, which was subject to censorship, remained slow). Another of Uhlman's few extant observations on life at Ascot concerned the beginnings – and these on the very first day – of collective cultural and educational activity there: an impromptu French class, an English class, small groups of men clustering around a 'lecturer', even an actor reciting from Goethe's *Faust*. 'The system of self-preservation by learning had begun,' wrote Uhlman[19] – and while this was a phenomenon that could be observed in each of the civilian internment camps, then nowhere more so than in Hutchinson which, according to ex-inmate Ronald Stent, was 'full of once and future Very Important Persons'.[20]

Hutchinson Camp was opened on 13 July 1940 and was one of a number of civilian camps established around the Isle of Man in Douglas, Ramsey, Onchan, Peel and, for women, in Port Erin and Port St Mary. By the end of July there were around 1,200 men interned in Hutchinson, mostly Jewish refugees but with non-Jewish internees forming a sizeable minority.[21] Some of the latter were political exiles, some 'Aryan' Germans who had lived in Britain for years but had omitted to apply for naturalization, while a few would have been National Socialist sympathizers. Most of the internees arrived, like Uhlman, from the transit camp in which they were initially held.

Hutchinson Camp, in Douglas, was made up of around forty boarding houses forming two rows around Hutchinson Square and of a third parallel row, the whole of it being enclosed in barbed wire. The square itself, which was positioned on a slope, was planted out with lawns, flowers and shrubs, and offered a very fine view of the sea. The houses, which had previously been used for the holiday trade, consisted of a large dining room, also serving as a lounge, a kitchen and bathroom, and around eight bedrooms, most of them furnished with two double beds, and thus room for four internees in each. These sleeping arrangements represented a source of difficulty from the beginning, with most internees refusing to share a bed, preferring rather to separate the mattress from the bed frame, thereby doubling the sleeping area. Even though this resulted in severe congestion in the bedrooms, and despite other shortcomings of the accommodation, the conditions were still generally much better in Hutchinson than they had been in the primitive transit camps.[22]

Within the barbed wire, the camp was largely administered by the internees themselves, though under the overall control of the Commander, Captain (later Major) H.O. Daniel, a fair-minded and humane if intellectually rather bounded officer, who had worked for Unilever before the war. He was assisted by Sergeant-Major Potterton, a smartly turned out, jovial man who in civilian life was the Head Porter of the fashionable Dolphin Square apartment blocks in Westminster, and by the Intelligence Officer Lieutenant (later Captain) C.G. Jurgensen, a man of Norwegian extraction, who, unlike the Commander, had a command of several languages as well as an understanding both of the complexities of the German situation and of the refugees' position within it. Under them, internee self-administration was carried out by means of an elected 'Camp Father', working with a network of similarly elected 'Street Fathers' and 'House Fathers'. (The first Camp Father was the writer and journalist Friedrich Burschell who would soon describe his task in *The Camp*, the Hutchinson journal, as 'neither easy nor enjoyable' because, among other reasons, 'he has to deal with men who feel themselves treated unjustly and whose nerves are not at their best'.[23])

Since the hotel-keepers and staff had been required to leave their properties unattended, cleaning rotas had to be drawn up in each house and a cook appointed from among the residents, who then had to make what he could out of the daily rations allocated to him. In fact, some surprising culinary talents emerged from this system, with Hellmuth Weissenborn, graphic artist and ex-professor from the Academy of Graphic Arts in Leipzig, being deemed the best cook in the camp! Apart from these fairly minimal domestic duties, the only obligation for internees was the twice daily attendance at roll call, with the day being further punctuated by mealtimes (at 8.00, 12.30 and 6.30).

Clearly in these conditions it was important for camp morale that internees be kept usefully occupied, as the Commander was well aware. Indeed Daniel's ideal for his camp was that of the 'happy family', which many internees understandably found galling.[24] With Daniel's support, internees reportedly drew up five aims, nonetheless – the precise authorship and provenance of the document in which these are contained is unknown – that were intended to inform camp life and behaviour:

1. To be released so as to take part in the fight against Germany;
2. To use the time in internment to make internees fit for work in war industries, and to give them a thorough schooling in English and industrial technique [*sic*];
3. To make the time in Camp bearable and fill it with work to such extent that no breathing space was left for mourning and grumbling;
4. To maintain on a high level the internees' physical training and thus their state of health;
5. To create out of this emergency-community of interned refugees a real community.[25]

These aims were, in the view of the document's anonymous author, largely achieved in Hutchinson with the exception of the last; it had not, he maintained, proved possible to create that 'real community' because of the very divergent backgrounds of the internees. Yet, on a more superficial level perhaps, a genuine community life soon emerged behind the wire with the establishment of the camp post office, the hospital, the bank and the canteen and, within a week of the camp opening, the library. In the running of these and other common institutions as well as in the boarding houses, the internees, thrown together by their common fate, had perforce to collaborate.

At the same time, of course, in Hutchinson as in life outside the camp, the internees were quick to seek out other likeminded people, as Uhlman's Internment Diary and Memoir amply illustrate. And Hutchinson was certainly rich in its range of human talent, with its groups of academics, writers, industrialists, doctors, politicians, trades unionists, businessmen, aristocrats, graphologists, rabbis, Catholic and Protestant ministers, scientists, engineers and – in particularly abundant supply – artists. One of the best known of the Hutchinson internees was Rudolf Olden, the anti-Nazi lawyer, author and journalist, who during the warm days of July and August – the summer of 1940 was an exceptionally fine one – delivered political analyses to audiences of 300–400 on the lawns of Hutchinson Square. Klaus Hinrichsen, the art historian, later recalled:

> To be interned with Rudolf Olden was similar [to being] interned with James Cameron, somebody who has been everywhere, somebody who has interviewed all the great politicians and has a world-wide view and philosophic approach to everything.[26]

Indeed Olden, whose internment was singled out for especial critical comment in Parliament,[27] was released after only three weeks and, with a job awaiting him at the New School for Social Research in New York, left Britain in September 1940. Sadly, his ship, the *City of Benares*, was torpedoed in mid-Atlantic, its many casualties including Rudolf Olden and his wife Ika. Back in Hutchinson, the news of Olden's death was a cause of particular dismay, with Burschell, as Camp Father, attaching an appreciation of his life and work to the latest issue of *The Camp*.[28] A similar piece composed by the writer Heinrich Fraenkel included the fatalistic observation: 'The Nazis got him after all.'[29]

Fraenkel was a further Hutchinson celebrity who devoted his time in internment to writing his book, *Help us Germans to Beat the Nazis!*, published by Victor Gollancz in 1941. In this, he called on the British to enlist the help of the German exiles in anti-Nazi propaganda as well as to draw a clear distinction between Germans and Nazis. It is interesting to note that in Hutchinson, thanks to the Home Office and to Captain Daniel, Fraenkel was granted every facility to write his book, including a private room – a rare luxury – exemption from postal restrictions and delays, and the provision of the requisite books and papers, many of them National Socialist in tenor.[30]

Indeed, Captain Daniel, once he had realized the talent he had in his camp, took great pride in it and went out of his way to support intellectual and artistic endeavour. One of his charges was the pianist Maryan Rawicz who, as part of the double act Rawicz and Landauer, had previously performed to members of the British Royal Family. Notwithstanding the fact that Landauer was interned in a different camp, Daniel arranged for the two pianists to be reunited for a concert, even hiring two high quality pianos especially for the purpose.[31]

Kurt Schwitters, the Dadaist painter and poet, whom Uhlman mentions frequently in his memoir, was a further Hutchinson celebrity who received special support from the Commander. Although the culturally rather conservative Captain Daniel may be assumed to have had only a limited appreciation of Schwitters' porridge sculptures and canine imitations (though he was reported to have liked his portraits), the artist was provided with a studio in which to work, and had produced, by his release in November 1941, between two and three hundred pictures in Hutchinson.[32]

One of the camp institutions in which the Commander took the greatest pride was its Cultural Department, founded only a matter of days after the camp had come into being. Daniel himself enjoyed calling it the 'Camp University' and is said to have been delighted that his camp was superior in this regard to the rival Onchan Camp.[33] The original organizer was the architect Bruno Ahrends; he was succeeded after a few weeks by Klaus Hinrichsen who remained in this office until his release in June 1941. Hinrichsen has recorded that some of the internees initially opposed the idea of cultural activity in the camp for fear that inmates might thereby become reconciled to their lot; they considered that non-cooperation or passive resistance would be a more fruitful way by which to obtain release. However, an alternative, more pragmatic viewpoint, that was certainly more in keeping with the Hutchinson five aims, won the day: this maintained that it was vital to cheer the internees' spirits and boost morale, with cultural activity having a vital role to play here.[34]

Drawing on its resident talent, the Cultural Department began to put on lectures, concerts, classes, performances, debates and the like, at first outdoors in the square or in the dining rooms of the individual boarding houses, later on in the hall that was constructed by the internees themselves, with support from the Commander. The lecture provision was chaotic to start with, with lecturers competing for space on the lawn, and Ahrends soon recognized the necessity of drawing up a regular timetable and establishing a committee of house representatives to coordinate it.

Certain recurrent images feature in the memoirs of ex-Hutchinson internees that reflect above all the camp's rich cultural activity. One is of eminent lecturers, bathed in sunshine, addressing their students on the Hutchinson Square lawns, a scene that has been compared – and not entirely ironically – with Athens at the time of Socrates.[35] Another is of scores of internees carrying their chairs from one house to the next and from one lecture to another.[36] For, as the opening number of *The Camp* put it, there were lectures on offer 'of every description, on Socialism and Dadaism, Zionism and Metabolism'.[37] So popular were these events that even a lecture on Etruscology had to be repeated twice. And the range was certainly extraordinary, a veritable *'embarras de richesse'* as Uhlman vividly recalled in his autobiography, *The Making of An Englishman*:

> What could one do if Professor William Cohn's talk on the Chinese Theatre coincided with Egon Wellesz' Introduction to Byzantine Music? Or Professor Jacobsthal's talk on Greek Literature with Professor Goldmann's on the Etruscan Language? Perhaps one felt more inclined to hear Zuntz on the Odyssey or Friedenthal on the Shakespearean stage.[38]

Wellesz, the celebrated musicologist, in fact delivered six lectures between early August and his release in October, including the one mentioned here on Byzantine Music, his specialism.[39] The writer Richard Friedenthal observed later that, whereas previously in Wellesz' career such a lecture might have appealed only to a select audience, 'now he had three hundred or five hundred, you know, who eagerly discussed the finer points of Byzantine music'.[40]

Yet if Hutchinson possessed almost a surfeit of academics (and artists, as will be discussed below), there was a relative dearth of practising musicians as compared, for example, with Onchan or Central Promenade camps. Still, it could boast Maryan Rawicz, of course, as well as the renowned pianist Richard Glas and a few others, and regular concerts formed an important feature of camp life. A review in *The Camp* of a Glas performance testifies to the significance of such events for the internees: 'For one hour and in one room there is no war. The thrill and charm of beautiful music has banished it.'[41] Another concert, this one performed al fresco to an evidently very large audience was put on

> in front of the houses of the front row, when some were hanging out of the windows as in Italian operas, while the musicians played and sang on the front steps with the crowded audience in front of them on the lawns and right down the pavement, fascinating even outsiders beyond the wire.[42]

A cabaret group, the 'Stacheldrahtkabarett' (Barbed Wire Cabaret) was formed in the camp by the Austrian cabaret artist Peter Herz, and there was also a theatre group, the 'Players' Guild', in which professional actors like Fritz Weiss, the group leader, or Franz Boensch worked side by side with 'many remarkable talents among the amateurs'.[43] Although, until the hall was opened at Christmas 1940, staging could prove problematical, small-scale productions such as scenes from *A Midsummer Night's Dream* or from Kleist's *Der zerbrochene Krug* were put on in individual boarding houses. The hall was finally inaugurated with an ambitious production of Chesterton's *The Man Who Was Thursday*, featuring twenty different sets and around thirty actors on its rather small stage. By early 1942 it was calculated that, in all, forty performances had been given to audiences totalling around 7000, with a production of Robert Ardrey's antifascist play *Thunder Rock* being deemed the camp's theatrical highlight.[44] A noteworthy part of the cultural programme in Hutchinson was the camp's Debating Society, conceived along Oxford Union lines; its business was conducted solely in English and its aim 'to provide amusing practice in English debating without the passionate feeling of hatred against the opponent'[45] which was a skill considered important for an understanding of British democracy. Motions were proposed on such topics as 'It's better to have loved and lost than never to have loved at all' – political topics were excluded – and the debates proved an enjoyable part of camp life 'even if the accent was peculiar and the syntax sometimes slipping'.[46]

For the younger internees, that is for boys initially as young as sixteen (though the age limit for internment was raised to eighteen in the first White Paper), a Youth Group was set up which offered a variety of social, educational, dramatic and musical activities. In addition, a Technical School was established in which the Commander took an especial pride. This set out to train the young men, many of whom had had their education interrupted by exile or by internment, in technical and electrical skills, the curriculum including mathematics, physics, technical translation and English in addition to practical training. The School's chief purpose in all of this, according to its founder and organizer Dr Ludwig Max Warschauer, was to equip pupils 'to help England and to become useful members of the economic machine of this country'.[47] And indeed, unusually, its pupils were engaged in useful work even while in the camp, consisting of cleaving sheets of mica for use in valves and other electrical devices.

L.M. Warschauer, who was also the founder of the Language School, and to whom reference is made in a number of Hutchinson memoirs, emerges from the reports of his fellow internees as a mysterious and contradictory figure. It was rumoured that, while still in Germany, he had cooperated with the Gestapo on a system of electronic listening device, yet he was evidently extremely well connected in Britain, too, since he received official visits in the camp on a regular basis and engaged in confidential talks with his visitors. Despite his apparently Jewish surname, he denied that he was Jewish. He consistently expressed pro-British sympathies and let it be known from the start that, because of the important war work in which he was engaged, he was awaiting his imminent release.[48] British Security files, however, reveal rather more about Mr Warschauer: that he had been sent to Britain on an espionage mission in 1939 while posing as a refugee (although he was indeed Jewish), a fact he finally admitted under repeated MI5 interrogation. He was moved from Hutchinson, where he had worked his way into the position of 'Daniel's blue-eyed boy' and 'pet internee', but continued to be held in custody in the Oratory School, in Brixton Prison and back on the Isle of Man until the end of the war, being repatriated to Germany against his wish in December 1945.[49]

Despite its dubious founder, however, the Technical School was generally regarded as one of Hutchinson's strengths,[50] as were its bevy of internationally known academics and of course its artists. For, quite apart from Fred Uhlman and Kurt Schwitters, other artists interned in the camp included Georg Ehrlich, Ernst Müller-Blensdorf, Siegfried Charoux, Paul Hamann, Fritz Krämer, the graphic artist-turned-cook Hellmuth Weissenborn, Hermann Fechenbach, Fritz Solomonski, the stage designer E.E. Stern, Erich Kahn and, for a time, Ludwig Meidner, all in all an astonishing array of talent. In a series of articles in *The Camp*, Klaus Hinrichsen described how, undeterred by a shortage of materials, the artists set about engaging in 'a new branch of the graphical arts' that consisted of scratching images on the boarding house windows (which had been painted blue in lieu of blackout curtains). House no. 28, for example, where Weissenborn lived, was soon named the 'House of Fairy Tales' because of the mythical creatures adorning its windows, house no. 19 was the 'House of the Bathing Girls', while no. 40, which had been engraved with animal images by the trapper and lion-tamer Mr Neunzer – happily a photograph of Neunzer's window has survived – was named the 'Zoo House'.[51]

As with other cultural endeavours within his camp, the Commander supported his artists enthusiastically: they even had an 'artists' café' at their disposal in a basement laundry room, where the painters and sculptors could meet. It was here, incidentally, that the letter to the *New Statesman and Nation* was drafted that was signed by seventeen German and Austrian artists, including Uhlman. 'Art cannot live behind barbed wire,' they asserted, before concluding with an appeal to British colleagues and others to help them obtain their liberty.[52]

Two art exhibitions, moreover, were put on in the camp, the first of them in September 1940, the second two months later. The latter, at which the artists were permitted to sell their own work – and indeed many paintings were sold – featured sculpture and craft work as well as paintings. Hinrichsen has recalled of the opening of the second exhibition that it 'had all the trappings of a professional art gallery with Private View invitations, a catalogue and speeches by the Camp Father and the Commander', as well as a concluding performance of chamber music.[53] The Camp Father, while thanking the Commander for his help and understanding, also took the opportunity to point to the difficult circumstances in which the artists had produced their work, and to the fact that they, and indeed all the internees, could be contributing to the British war effort if only they were at liberty.[54] The Commander, for his part, reportedly confined himself to 'a few friendly words' before declaring the exhibition open.[55]

A similar exchange of addresses also marked the appearance of *The Camp* whose opening number, produced on a duplicator, appeared on 21 September 1940. Its editor was Michael Freund-Corvin, formerly on the editorial staff of the celebrated *Berliner Tageblatt* and a survivor of the *Arandora Star*. The whole of the front page was made up of the two complementary pieces, the

'Commander's Introduction' and the 'Campfathers [*sic*] Introduction', the former listing the Hutchinson achievements to date – such as the Technical School, first art exhibition and so on – culminating in the publication of the newspaper itself. The Camp Father, on the other hand, portrayed the publication of *The Camp*, though still in a positive light, as a means of mirroring the internees' difficult situation and of making it more bearable.

The newspaper had an important informatory function, enabling camp organizations such as the Cultural Department, the Youth Group or the Technical College to advertise their activities. In addition, a 'Letters to the Editor' column provided a forum for the discussion of issues of camp life, including the function of the camp paper itself. A letter in the second issue, for instance, from 'A Friend', criticized *The Camp*'s opening number for being intended more for opinion outside the camp – 'draussen' – than for the internees themselves. (Although *The Camp*'s policy was to publish in English, this letter, exceptionally, appeared in German, thereby lending additional weight to the writer's point.)[56]

Space was regularly given over to 'Commander's Announcements': in the third issue, for instance, Daniel informed the readership of the new camp loudspeaker system, the provision of beer in the canteen and the fact that the eagerly anticipated new hall was under construction, while at the same time warning his charges against the possible presence in their midst of 'the Grumbler, the Shirker and [...] the Rumour Monger'.[57] In exchange, the paper also provided a useful channel for communicating internee concerns back to the Commander. Thus the fourth issue carried an editorial entitled 'Open Letter to the Commander' which made a plea for internees to be permitted to work for the war effort: 'Will you please help us by allowing us to help the country.'[58] Other serious matters addressed in the columns of *The Camp* included, in issue no. 2, the internees' need to defend themselves against the 'ridiculous and brutal attacks' that had been made against them from outside the camp, for instance by the *Isle of Man Times*,[59] and, in no. 3, the subject of release from internment. Readers had been demanding that *The Camp* adopt a more aggressive stance on the matter; in its editorial, however, the newspaper warned that this could prove counterproductive, advising instead: 'We have to look on this time as a test [...] of endurance, patience and loyalty. Let us consider ourselves a silent reserve, steady and in spite of all difficulties sure and quiet.'[60]

In addition, *The Camp* carried material that reflected Hutchinson's rich cultural life: reviews of exhibitions, lectures, concerts and dramatic performances; articles such as the five-part series by Klaus Hinrichsen on the camp's window paintings; and, in no. 5, the announcement of an essay competition on the subject, 'One Day in Hutchinson Camp' (the prizes were later awarded to a Dr Mero for an essay entitled 'An Adventurous Day' and to G. Hirschfeld for his 'Present and Future').[61] The first cartoon by Dol (probably A. Mierecki) appeared in the second issue.[62] Thereafter, a number of Hutchinson artists mastered the technique of drawing on stencil, including Uhlman, two of whose drawings – one of the camp itself, the other of a seascape – appeared in *The Camp*'s Christmas double number, *Almanac 1940–1941*, which featured work of the Hutchinson artists and writers while also reflecting on the preceding six months of camp life.[63]

Yet, despite all this productive activity, the difficulties of life in internment – of confinement, fear, anxiety and homesickness – should not be underestimated. Indeed the problems of internment ranged from major issues – such as the fear that, in the event of a German invasion of Britain, refugees on the Isle of Man would present all too easy a target – to relatively minor difficulties that could nevertheless cast a blight on everyday living. Paul Jacobsthal, in his memoir, recalls, for instance, the problem of enforced familiarity for 'strangers sentenced to intimacy of meals and bed'.[64] A further issue for many, as remembered by Klaus Hinrichsen, was their loss of status: 'It was quite a job to persuade people that now they were internees and they were no longer Herr Geheimrat or Herr Rittmeister.'[65]

Moreover internment commonly had the effect of exacerbating the feelings of dislocation, disorientation and loss already engendered by the experience of exile. The loss that Jacobsthal, for one, regretted most bitterly in British exile was that of the 'Muttersprache', of his native tongue.[66] It is interesting to note in this connection, however, that in Hutchinson as a whole opinions differed on the language most appropriate for common use. Hellmuth Weissenborn, for instance, whose English was evidently already quite good, recounts that he nevertheless opposed the suggestion that English should become the lingua franca in his boarding house, on the grounds that residents would be bound to descend into 'refugee English'.[67] Fritz Hallgarten, on the other hand, recalls that 'everybody made an effort to speak English' in his house, even if 'pidgin English' frequently resulted.[68] Camp announcements were, of course, issued in English; and, as mentioned above, the policy both of the Debating Society and, generally speaking, of the camp journal was to use English as a mark of loyalty to the British cause. As Klaus Hinrichsen explains: 'It would be a bad idea [...] to go on speaking and using German if you claimed to the War Office and the Home Office that you considered yourself prospective Englishmen and people who were fighting the Germans.'[69] And there were, indeed, some internees who, as a political gesture, refused to speak or read any German at all, even though their English was far from perfect. However, Hinrichsen also tells the story of the Intelligence Officer, Captain Jurgensen, whose task it was to censor the outgoing mail, and who requested the letter writers kindly to write in German, since 'he could understand it so much better than their English'.[70]

In Hutchinson, as in the other alien internment camps, the deprivations of internment were particularly keenly felt at Christmas time because of inevitable associations with home, family and happier days. By December 1940, numerous internees had been released, compounding the emotionalism of the experience for those left behind. Uhlman, for one, was moved to recall in his Internment Memoir the beauty of the traditional German Christmas, even while fully aware of the anomalous nature of his response (that of a non-believer who, in the normal course of events, did not enjoy Christmas).[71] Schwitters, too, would relate to his wife that he had been unable to join in the Christmas carols for fear of weeping.[72] (As things turned out, Uhlman remained in internment for only a matter of days thereafter, but Schwitters was interned until almost the end of 1941.)

In the Post Scriptum to his Memoir, Uhlman attempts to draw up a balance sheet of the whole internment experience. On the one hand, the negative aspects: arrest, separation from his highly pregnant wife, humiliation, confusion and so on. On the other, the positive points: the exceptional cultural life, the friendship, courage and humour he encountered, and 'even sometimes the fun and the realization that this was a unique experience and that one could be proud to belong to an elite of the human race'. Klaus Hinrichsen, indeed, who in general takes a more uniformly positive view of the experience than Uhlman, singles out the companionship, the mixed company, and the unaccustomed freedom for artists to devote themselves entirely to their work. Internment, Hinrichsen concludes, was 'a great experience, really an experience [of] a lifetime'.[73] It is important, however, to set against that the largely unnecessary suffering that the British policy of indiscriminate civilian internment caused for many, as well as the fact, as concluded by the unsigned report on Hutchinson from early 1942, that it was a 'waste of both time and material' to intern people who could have represented a valuable asset to the war effort.[74]

Although Hutchinson Camp – renamed P Camp in mid-1941 – remained open until 1944, its composition became rather different from the early days of mass internment, including as time went on some Japanese internees and, later still, a few prisoners of war. Nevertheless, unlike other internment camps in the later period, which contained many Germans and Austrians loyal to the Reich, P Camp continued to be reserved for political internees and to pride itself on its predominantly antifascist stance.[75] And certainly, if one had to be interned, this camp, described as a 'Musterlager', or model camp, in a report compiled in November 1940 by visiting representatives from the Swiss Legation,[76] was a better place to be than most, at least for those internees of an antifascist disposition.

Life in Hutchinson Camp in these early days has been perpetuated in semi-fictional form by Richard Friedenthal in his aptly named novel *Die Welt in der Nussschale* (The World in a Nutshell).[77] Adopting a deliberately humorous stance, though with a number of characters clearly identifiable – Baby Bitters as Kurt Schwitters and the sinister Schlick as Warschauer, for instance – Friedenthal set out to portray 'the growing up of a community among very special conditions'.[78] Some of the friendships that were forged in internment lasted a lifetime; but in general, once the 'special conditions' that had bound internees together no longer obtained, friends drifted apart. Uhlman concludes his Internment Memoir with a visit to some ex-Hutchinsonians and former companions, the Professors Wellesz, Jacobsthal and Cohn, now back in Oxford, who were all 'very friendly, but very professional, very distinguished'. 'We were,' so he observes with maybe a hint of regret and – even thirty-eight years on – in slightly precarious English, 'no more in the same boat'.[79]

NOTES

1. Standard works on the internment of aliens in Britain in the Second World War include F. Lafitte, *The Internment of Aliens* (Harmondsworth: Penguin, 1940); Peter and Leni Gillman, *'Collar the Lot!' How Britain Interned and Expelled its Wartime Refugees* (London/Melbourne/New York: Quartet, 1980); Ronald Stent, *A Bespattered Page? The Internment of 'His Majesty's Most Loyal Enemy Aliens'* (London: André Deutsch, 1980); Michael Seyfert, *Im Niemandsland: Deutsche Exilliteratur in britischer Internierung: Ein unbekanntes Kapitel der Kulturgeschichte des Zweiten Weltkriegs* (Berlin: Das Arsenal, 1984); and David Cesarani and Tony Kushner (eds), *The Internment of Aliens in Twentieth Century Britain* (London: Frank Cass, 1993). For the internment of women, see Charmian Brinson, '"In the exile of internment" or "Von Versuchen aus einer Not eine Tugend zu machen": German-speaking women interned by the British during the Second World War', in William Niven and James Jordan (eds), *Politics and Culture in Twentieth Century Germany* (Rochester, NY: Camden House, 2003).
2. Figure given by Sir John Anderson in the House of Commons on 1 February 1940 (*Hansard*, HC, vol. 356, col. 1270).
3. According to the written answer supplied by Sir John Anderson on 1 March 1940 (see *Hansard*, HC, vol. 357, col. 2410). According to this, there were in addition 6,782 'B' and 64,244 'C' categorizations (although different figures were cited from time to time by other official spokesmen).
4. Dated 14 May 1940, held at National Archives [NA], FO 371/25189. In addition, Bland expanded on his report in a BBC broadcast on 30 May 1940.
5. G. Ward Price, 'There is More to be Done', *Daily Mail*, 24 May 1940, p.4.
6. See E.M. Forster *et al.*, 'Interning Aliens', *The Times*, 23 July 1940, p.5.
7. H.G. Wells, 'J'Accuse', *Reynolds News*, 28 July 1940, p.6.
8. Michael Foot, 'Why not lock up General de Gaulle?', *Evening Standard*, 17 July 1940, p.5.
9. *Hansard*, HC, vol. 362, cols. 1207–1306, 10 July 1940.
10. *Hansard*, HL, vol. CXVI, col. 544, 12 June 1940.
11. See Cmd. 6217.
12. *Civilian Internees of Enemy Nationality*, August 1940, Cmd. 6223.
13. *Civilian Internees of Enemy Nationality (Revised)*, October 1940, Cmd. 6233.
14. On this, see Stent, *A Bespattered Page?*, pp.201 f.
15. Paul Jacobsthal, 'The Long Vac 1940', in R.M. Cooper (ed.), *Refugee Scholars: Conversations with Tess Simpson* (Leeds: Morland Books, 1992), p.226.
16. See, for example, Uhlman Internment Memoir, 26 October 1940; Jacobsthal, 'The Long Vac 1940', p.227.
17. As cited in Yvonne Kapp and Margaret Mynatt, *British Policy and the Refugees, 1933–1941* (London: Frank Cass, 1997), p.135.
18. *Hansard*, HC, vol. 368, cols. 1503–04.
19. Uhlman Internment Memoir, 26 June 1940.
20. Stent, *A Bespattered Page?*, p.172.
21. An unpublished paper from the time by W.G. Feuchtwang, 'Hutchinson Camp, July–December 1940, some figures', gives the following breakdown for the camp population in the early months: c. 1,050 Jews, 100 Protestants and 50–60 Catholics (ms. in private possession of Stefan Feuchtwang, London).
22. Apart from the sources already cited, information on Hutchinson Camp given here and below is based largely on interviews in the Imperial War Museum's series 'Civilian Internment in Britain 1939–1945' with former Hutchinsonians Fred Uhlman, Hellmuth Weissenborn, Richard Friedenthal, Peter Midgley, Fritz Hallgarten and Klaus Hinrichsen; on Klaus Hinrichsen's 'Visual Arts behind the Wire' in Cesarani and Kushner (eds), *The Internment of Aliens*; on the Hutchinson journal, *The Camp*, 1940–41; and on an unsigned 39-page document from early 1942, '"P" Camp, Douglas, Isle of Man', held at Imperial War Museum [IWM], Misc. 188/Item 2843.
23. Fredric [*sic*] Burschell, 'Camp Father's task', *The Camp*, no. 5 (20 October 1940), p.1.
24. Jacobsthal, 'The Long Vac 1940', p.216.
25. '"P" Camp, Douglas, Isle of Man', p.3.
26. Interview with Klaus Hinrichsen, 'Civilian Internment in Britain 1939–1945', IWM,

Department of Sound Records, 003789, p.53.
27. For instance by George Strauss and Wilfrid Roberts on 10 July 1940 (*Hansard*, HC, vol. 362, cols. 1260 and 1265).
28. Frederic [*sic*] Burschell, 'Rudolf Olden', on sheet attached to p.1 of *The Camp*, no. 2 (29 September 1940).
29. Heinrich Fraenkel, 'In Memoriam Rudolf Olden', in *Almanac 1940–1941* (i.e., nos. 13–14 of *The Camp*), December 1940, p.10. See also Heinrich Fraenkel, *Help Us Germans To Beat the Nazis!* (London: Gollancz, 1941), pp.116–17. In the light of these and similar appreciations of Olden's life and work, Uhlman's later question 'Who was Olden?' (Internment Memoir, question appended to entry of 24 September 1940) is surprising.
30. See Fraenkel, *Help Us Germans To Beat the Nazis!*, p.104.
31. Interview with Fritz Hallgarten, 'Civilian Internment in Britain 1939–1945', IWM, Department of Sound Records, 003967, pp.40–41.
32. See Kurt Schwitters to Helma Schwitters, 21 November 1941, reproduced in Seyfert, *Im Niemandsland*, p.188.
33. See, for example, Hinrichsen Interview, p.29.
34. Klaus Hinrichsen, 'Cultural Flashlights', *Almanac 1940–1941*, p.29.
35. See, for example, Klaus Hinrichsen, 'Cultural Department, Hutchinson Internment Camp', statement dated 22 March 1988, IWM E88/294.
36. See, for example, Fred Uhlman, *The Making of an Englishman* (London: Gollancz, 1960), p.233. Uhlman comments further: 'The memory of all these men in pursuit of knowledge is one of the most moving and encouraging that I brought back from the strange microcosm in which I lived for so many months.'
37. 'The Cultural Department: To the Newcomers', *The Camp*, no. 1 (21 September 1940), p.7.
38. Uhlman, *The Making of an Englishman*, pp.232–3.
39. See Peter Revers, '"Es war nicht leicht, sich in die völlig veränderten Verhältnisse einzugewöhnen": Egon Wellesz' Emigrationsjahre in Oxford', in Friedrich Stadler (ed.), *Vertriebene Vernunft*, vol. II: *Emigration und Exil österreichischer Wissenschaft* (Vienna/Munich: Jugend und Volk, 1988), pp.619–20.
40. Interview with Richard Friedenthal, 'Civilian Internment in Britain 1939–1945', IWM, Department of Sound Records, 003963, p.30.
41. Medicus, 'Thoughts at a Camp Concert', *The Camp*, no. 4 (15 October 1940), p.6.
42. Perlmann, 'Music Review', *Almanac 1940–1941*, p.33.
43. '"P" Camp Douglas, Isle of Man', IWM, Misc 188/Item 2843, p.15.
44. Ibid., p.16.
45. 'The Cultural Department', *The Camp*, no. 1 (21 September 1940), p.8.
46. Stent, *A Bespattered Page?*, p.176.
47. L. Warschauer, 'Technical School', *Almanac 1940–1941*, p.20.
48. See, for example, Stent, *A Bespattered Page?*, p.176.
49. See National Archives, Kew [NA], KV2/1139-1142.
50. Though see Hinrichsen Interview, according to which the pupils, who spent their time splitting mica, were thereby prevented from receiving a more general education and indeed were 'really exploited' (p.38).
51. See Klaus Hinrichsen, 'Nail, Knife and Razor-Blade: The Windows of the Camp', in *The Camp*, no. 6 (27 October 1940), p.3; no. 7 (3 November 1940), p.3; no. 8 (13 November 1940), p.2; no. 9 (17 November 1940), p.3; and no. 10 (24 November 1940), p.2. A photograph of Neunzer and his window is reproduced in Cesarani and Kushner (eds), *The Internment of Aliens*, p.191.
52. 'Refugees', *New Statesman and Nation*, 24 August 1940, pp.185–6.
53. Hinrichsen, 'Visual Arts Behind the Wire', p.200.
54. 'The Campfathers [*sic*] address to the Commander on Occasion of the Opening of the Second Art Exhibition', *The Camp*, no. 10 (24 November 1940), p.1.
55. Hinrichsen, 'Visual Arts Behind the Wire', p. 200.
56. 'Letters to the Editor', *The Camp*, no. 2 (29 September 1940), p.8.
57. 'Commander's Announcements', *The Camp*, no. 3 (6 October 1940), p.2.
58. *The Camp*, no. 4 (15 October 1940), p.1. For the Commander's reaction, see Uhlman's Internment Diary entry of 16 October 1940.
59. 'Review', *The Camp*, no. 2 (29 September 1940), p.1. This is probably a reference to readers'

letters and to editorial comment in the *Isle of Man Daily Times* earlier in September 1940 concerning the public concert that internees had intended to give in aid of Noble's Hospital. This concert had to be cancelled because of public protest.
60. 'Realism', *The Camp*, no. 3 (6 October 1940), p.1.
61. The winning essays were published in *The Camp*, no. 8 (13 November 1940), pp.9–10, and no. 10 (24 November 1940), p. 8.
62. Entitled 'Invasion', *The Camp*, no. 2 (29 September 1940), p.5.
63. According to the editor's and administrator's 'Preface and Thanks', p.3, the aim of *Almanac 1940–1941* was 'to achieve a cross section through the cultural and artistic life of Hutchinson Camp in the second half of the year 1940'. Uhlman's drawings are on pp.7 and 22.
64. Jacobsthal, 'The Long Vac 1940', p.225.
65. Hinrichsen Interview, p.23.
66. Jacobsthal, 'The Long Vac 1940', p.225.
67. Weissenborn Interview, pp.23 f.
68. Hallgarten Interview, p.35.
69. Hinrichsen Interview, pp.29 f.
70. Ibid., p.30.
71. Uhlman Internment Memoir, 24–25 December 1940.
72. Kurt Schwitters to Helma Schwitters, 24 December 1940, reproduced in Seyfert, *Im Niemandsland*, p.183.
73. Hinrichsen Interview, p.34.
74. '"P" Camp, Douglas, Isle of Man', p.39.
75. See, for example, report on a visit to the camp on 8 May 1942 by representatives of the Swiss Legation which recorded the presence of only seven Germans professing allegiance to the Reich out of a population of 349 (Politisches Archiv des Auswärtigen Amtes, Berlin [AA], R42017). See also report on a visit on 9 February 1944 by J. Wirth of the International Red Cross Committee, 'Camp P, Ile de Man', NA, FO 916/846.
76. AA, R41798.
77. First published by Piper in Munich, 1956. It has never appeared in English.
78. Friedenthal Interview, p.33.
79. Uhlman Internment Memoir, 'Post Scriptum'.

3. *Fred Uhlman and the Croft Connection*

Anna Müller-Härlin

When, in April 1936, the refugee artist Fred Uhlman fell in love with the Englishwoman Diana Croft in Spain, it changed his situation as an émigré dramatically. By the time he arrived in Spain, Uhlman was unsure as to how he was going to continue his life in exile. After the three years in France, during which he had relied on his savings, his financial resources were now beginning to dwindle. He knew that he wanted to devote his life to painting but was uncertain as to how he should earn his living. He was also unsure as to whether he should stay in Spain or return to France. He decided on the latter, however, after spending three months in the fishing village Tossa del Mar,[1] because of the outbreak of the Spanish Civil War. In August, Diana and Fred met up in Paris, and they decided that he should join her in England. He arrived in London a month later and they got married in November 1936.

Uhlman later maintained that, in bringing him to England, Diana had saved his life.[2] Indeed, had he not emigrated to England, it could have had devastating consequences: if he had remained in France, like so many other refugees, he could have been arrested by the occupying power in May 1940 and deported to a German concentration camp. Hypothetically, then, Diana did indeed save Uhlman's life. What can be definitely asserted is that the decision to join Diana in England and to marry her, changed Uhlman's life entirely. Without Diana, Uhlman would certainly not have been able to live as a painter, because, as he put it himself, it was she who 'allowed me to work without financial worries. In this sense, everything I have done has been done by her'.[3] Their son Francis Uhlman explains: 'She gave him a roof over his head, [...] and she gave him credibility and status.'[4] Due to Diana's financial position – she once joked that 'I have a little bit more money than a real Socialist should possess!'[5] – the Uhlmans were able to buy their house in Hampstead, 47 Downshire Hill, in September 1938. It was also because of Diana's financial independence that the Uhlman family did not have to rely on Uhlman's career as an artist.[6] The fact that he had no need to worry about money from his very first day in England onwards distinguished Uhlman from most other exiles. Due to Diana, Uhlman was also able to mix in British society far more easily than many other refugees arriving on this island, and his inclusion in elevated English social circles also had an influence on Uhlman's career.[7]

Diana Croft was born on 31 March 1912 as the second daughter of Nancy Beatrice Borwick and Sir Henry Page Croft. She had three siblings: two sisters, Elizabeth and Rosemary (called Posy), and a brother, Michael.[8] The Croft family was descended from Bernard de Croft, who was mentioned in the Domesday Survey of 1086. From 1296 until 1727, members of the Croft family were almost continuously represented in Parliament. Apart from their long tradition of parliamentary service, Diana's ancestors had occupied various prestigious posts. They had, for example, held the bishopric of Hereford under Charles II and had served the Royal Family: in the early nineteenth century, Sir Richard Croft had been summoned as physician to the deathbed of the daughter of the Prince Regent.[9]

Diana's father, Brigadier-General Sir Henry Page Croft (1881–1947) was appointed first Baron Croft in 1940.[10] Croft was a well-known Conservative politician who belonged to the Party's extreme right-wing. Between 1910 and 1918, he was MP for Christchurch; and was then MP for Bournemouth until 1940. He was fiercely nationalistic and entirely devoted to the defence of the British Empire and to the maintenance of its colonies. When in 1903 Joseph Chamberlain launched his imperial crusade against free trade, Croft was a strong supporter and became involved in the Tariff Reform League, of which he was chairman from 1913 to 1917.[11] He also became a member of a secret organization called the Confederacy, which sought to campaign against Conservative Party members in favour of free trade.[12] So well known were his radical politics regarding the British colonies that the news of the marriage of Diana and Uhlman was, in fact, used against him by the National Socialist newspaper, *Stuttgarter Nachrichten*. In Uhlman's home town, the marriage was interpreted as yet another sign of the Jewish world conspiracy in which Uhlman was cast as a conspirator, in control of Croft's political aspirations to strengthen British power in the colonies: 'The political colonial forays against Germany of the very honourable Sir Henry Page Croft now have a natural explanation.'[13]

In 1917, Croft's nationalism was behind the founding of his own party with the aim of strengthening the Empire. He returned to the Conservative Party in 1923 after his National Party had folded. In May 1940, he joined Churchill's Cabinet as Under-Secretary of State for War. All his life Croft remained active for the imperial cause. From 1924 until his death in 1947, he was chairman of the Empire Industries Association, a body which endeavoured to support British commerce.[14]

Diana's sister Posy Poole has recalled the 'almost Edwardian upbringing' of the Croft children in Onslow Gardens in South Kensington and at Knole, Bournemouth. At the age of six or seven, Diana was sent to a preparatory boarding school, and at the age of eleven to St James's School, Malvern. She was considered an extremely difficult child, non-conformist and always 'rebellious' in everything she did.[15]

Posy Poole has summarized her parents' attitude to their daughters as follows: 'They need no education, they should be civilized but they need not know about maths or physics.'[16] In line with the traditional concept of women as unsuited to the sciences and as merely fit for marriage, Diana was sent to finishing schools in both Paris and Florence. She did extremely well there, and also improved her language skills. A very talented linguist, she had already won a significant prize for her French.[17] Upon her return to London, Diana did the season, but she did not marry as was expected of her and was then sent off to India for some months to stay with friends of the family.[18] Back in London, much to the annoyance of her parents, she worked in a hospital for six months and undertook secretarial training. She also spent some time in Munich learning to sing with a German countess.[19] Singing seems to have been a considerable passion of hers and she made a private recording of Schubert songs.[20] In a letter of June 1936, written to Uhlman while he was still in Tossa, Diana informed him that she was looking for a flat in

London where she could work and pursue her singing career.[21] Written in German (as well as partly in French), the letter reveals Diana's excellent language skills, her German displaying a charming Southern influence.

Posy Poole has stated that Diana, being the enterprising rebel that she was, became 'automatically left-wing' as a young woman. This stance had evolved from a reaction against her upper-class background, as well as a rebellion against her parents with whom her relationship had generally been very negative.[22] She soon enthusiastically inflicted her left-wing ideas on her younger siblings who used to read Marx in their nursery, admiring their older sister greatly.

Diana travelled through France and Spain with her friend, Betty Sackville-West,[23] in Diana's Lagonda motorcar,[24] and this is also how they visited Tossa del Mar and met Uhlman. Diana's son has described the women as being 'political groupies' in many ways,[25] since they also experienced considerable excitement at visiting a region that stood on the brink of a civil war.[26]

After Diana had married Uhlman, she plunged into remarkable projects. Never in need of a job financially (Diana always worked on an unpaid basis), she possessed an indefatigable will in pursuit of voluntary work for countless good causes. In 1938, she became one of the driving forces behind the Artists' Refugee Committee. After the war, from 1947 until 1957, she played a leading role in the Artists' International Association.[27] From 1955 onwards, Diana turned her attention to another cause, namely the rescuing of her family's estate, Croft Castle in Herefordshire. Owing to disagreements within the family, the castle, which dates from around the fourteenth century, was running the risk of demolition. Diana organized the financial support to save the building from destruction.[28] The castle was from then on run by the National Trust; and Diana created a most impressive garden there. In 1987, two years after Uhlman's death, she sold 47 Downshire Hill and moved permanently to Croft Castle, living there until her death in 1999. Posy Poole found it strange that Diana, at one time such a rebel against the Establishment, should have become so interested in her family history while Francis Uhlman explained the behaviour of his mother in her later years as follows: 'And then she became the English aristocrat that she'd forgotten that she was. So she completely did a full circle.'[29]

For Diana, falling in love with Uhlman was the embodiment of her rebellious stance. Uhlman represented the counterpart to the social class to which she belonged but with which she did not identify. By marrying Uhlman, a penniless socialist German Jew pursuing an artistic career, she was embracing all of the attributes her family, and in particular her father, detested. According to her father, this amounted to 'social suicide'.[30] However, Diana stood by her husband and, as became particularly apparent during the period of Uhlman's internment, endured her father's political prejudices stoically. She retained her private income, however (which was derived from a trust set up by her maternal grandfather), and Lord Croft never behaved rudely towards Uhlman (who had had to endure being formally interviewed by Croft before the marriage, a scene that is very humorously recorded in Uhlman's autobiography). However, Croft never forgave Uhlman for marrying his daughter; after the marriage, Lord Croft kept his contact with the Uhlmans to a minimum.[31]

Thus Uhlman represented everything Lord Croft despised, politically as well as socially. Describing him as one of those 'rare phenomena in British political life: a rebel of the Right', the historian W.L. Guttsman has stated that Croft was 'a believer in the British "race", something of a xenophobe and somewhat lukewarm in his defence of Parliamentary democracy'.[32] As already indicated, defending the British race, in his eyes the 'greatest nation on earth', and the interests of the Empire were his major concerns.[33] As a corollary to this, Croft was fiercely anti-German. In 1915, he had been one of the co-founders of the British Empire Union (BEU), an organization which considered its major purpose to be the arousing of anti-German sentiment. Their activities would range from calls for the boycott of German products and employees to an aggressive strategy demanding the closure of German firms in Britain.[34] One of the National Party's credos during its existence from 1917 until 1923 was the 'eradication of German influence' in England.[35] In 1920, this xenophobic attitude led Croft to propose that 'for ten years no German should be allowed to live in this country'.[36]

Another major concern of the National Party was the supposed threat from the Bolshevists – with reference to the situation in Russia in 1919, Croft had published an article in the *Morning Post*, in which he concluded that the oligarchy there consisted mainly of 'Bolshevik German Jews who have come to Russia with German passports, [and have] established themselves as a government'.[37] In 1919, he let the *Daily Graphic* know that: 'Nearly all the sowers of Bolshevism were and are aliens and at most of their meetings Yiddish is spoken.'[38] Of course, Lord Croft was not alone in upholding such blatant anti-Semitic views: Tony Kushner has pointed out that in the 1930s and 1940s most people in Britain 'saw the Jews, even British-born Jews, as somehow foreign'.[39] The upper classes, in particular, considered foreign Jews a threat to the stability of British society. In conservative circles, especially, Jews were equated with radical and revolutionary behaviour.[40]

An incident which occurred as late as 1945 points to Croft's continuing prejudice against Jews. Croft had referred ironically to the Labour Party politician, Harold Laski, as 'a fine representative of the old British working class'. His comment was criticized by his friend, Winston Churchill, who admonished Croft as follows: 'Pray be careful, whatever the temptation, not to be drawn into any campaign that might be represented as anti-Semitism.'[41] Croft's answer to Churchill is revealing: grateful for the latter's warning, he explained that he had always been 'impressed with the danger of anti-Semitism and [I] have never mentioned the word Jew on the platform, other than to express sympathy with them'.[42] He thus at least indirectly confirmed his biased attitude towards Jews in considering them as 'other'.

In his memoirs written shortly before his death in 1947 and published in 1948, Lord Croft maintained his xenophobic standpoint. In the chapter 'After Munich', he described the disgust he had felt towards a 'very ugly crowd overwhelmingly foreign in appearance', who had demonstrated in London against the Munich Agreement and Chamberlain's policy. This crowd, he claimed, had shouted 'Shamberlain must go!'[43] Croft was, of course, both mimicking the accents of German-speaking refugees and categorizing them as trouble-makers. His perception of the Munich Agreement as a successful political undertaking was one thing, but his opinion that refugees were behind the destruction of hopes for peace quite another. It is particularly striking in light of the fact that this was written after 1945.[44]

The unbridgeable political divide between Lord Croft, on the one hand, and the Uhlmans on the other is best reflected in their differing political standpoints on the Spanish Civil War. While Uhlman was a Social Democratic Party member and Diana referred to herself as a 'real Socialist', Croft supported Franco and despised the Second Republic. Croft was, of course, not alone within the Conservative Right in supporting the Nationalists.[45] With his anti-German attitude, he was, in fact, a perfect example of the fact that those British politicians who were pro-Franco were not necessarily pro-Nazi. Rather, Croft's approval of Franco was fuelled by his hatred of Bolshevism. In October 1936, in a letter to *The Times*, Croft expressed his belief that the Civil War was 'widely organized by large numbers of agents imported from Moscow'.[46] With hindsight, Lord Croft stated in 1947 that he considered Franco's troops to have stood for the 'defence of Christianity and their Catholic faith, whereas the enemy was an army of destruction attempting to destroy everything that lingered of the old Spain, with nothing to put in its place except the destructive philosophy of Karl Marx'.[47] For these reasons, Croft 'never had the shadow of a doubt that the new Spain would emerge under General Franco's leadership', claiming that 'rarely in any war did a general show such wisdom'.[48] One of Croft's main arguments, which he repeatedly used against the Spanish Republicans, was that they were anti-Christian. In February 1937, he condemned the 'widespread and almost complete destruction of churches'[49] (alluding to attacks there by anarchists).[50] While Croft's outcry against 'anti-Christian' behaviour was most probably sincere, it can also be argued that the 'anti-Christian' argument was convenient when defending Franco's nationalist stance, since this was congruent with his own ideals.

While the Uhlmans were antifascists, Croft on the other hand was a member of an organization called the 'Friends of National Spain'.[51] He condemned those who held republican views in the House of Commons[52] and, in a pamphlet published by the 'Friends of National Spain' in 1937, he insisted that 'Conservatives can no longer remain silent', reassuring Franco that he 'can count on our moral support'.[53] In spring 1938, Croft pressed the Government through the British Foreign Secretary, Lord Halifax, to intervene in the Spanish Civil War by sending British ships from the Mediterranean to Barcelona to aid Franco. He even proposed to Halifax that English forces should be sent to Barcelona to 'protect life and property', on the assumption that the population would naturally welcome pro-Nationalists.[54] To this, Halifax – in line with Britain's non-interventionist policy[55] – dryly replied:

> Your proposal implies that the Spanish Government will be prepared to surrender Barcelona before their forces are actually driven out of it, whereas our evidence is to the effect that they are more likely to defend the city to the last.[56]

However, in February 1939 Halifax left no doubt that if victory were to be gained by Franco, Britain would immediately recognize his Government.[57] Croft was proud to record that he himself kept Franco informed of the political developments within the British Empire.[58] Although this direct contact was not mentioned in Halifax's letter, he nevertheless hinted that he was aware of Croft's role as a mediator, and of his close connections with Spanish Nationalists.

'SENTIMENT CANNOT RULE OUR ACTIONS'[59] – LORD CROFT AND INTERNMENT

When Uhlman was interned as an 'enemy alien', an anxious Diana approached her father for help. Lord Croft, then Under-Secretary of State for War in Churchill's Cabinet, did, indeed, address the Home Office on this matter. Concerned about his daughter's state of health (as she was about to give birth to her first child), and assuring the Home Office of his son-in-law's stance as 'anti-Hitler and well-affected to this country', his general approval of the Government's actions against 'enemy aliens', nevertheless, finds clear expression in his polite inquiry:

> Would you kindly let me know if this internment is general for German nationals in this category, or whether this action was taken in error [...] If this internment is general I have no comment to make.[60]

In July 1940, he wrote to the Home Office again on behalf of his daughter, who feared that Uhlman might be sent overseas. Under-Secretary Osbert Peake replied that:

> Arrangements have now been made to ensure that no internee who has a British-born wife will be sent overseas unless his wife is willing to accompany him. You may safely, therefore, give your daughter the assurance in this matter that she is so anxious to have.[61]

There is no record, however, that would testify to any attempt by Croft to speed up Uhlman's release despite the fact that his Cabinet post would have enabled him to mobilize forces to have his son-in-law released as quickly as possible. A desperate Uhlman himself then approached Croft in a letter, and since the latter had previously defended his son-in-law by giving testimony at the tribunal, he hoped to receive support from him.[62] However, his humble call for help did not soften Croft's standpoint. Although he did answer Uhlman's plea, he was not willing to interfere.[63] Writing to her husband from Bambers Green, Diana had clearly given up hope of her father's support:

> I don't think one can expect much more from Papa – his attitude is war is war – and the innocent must suffer with the guilty. I must get back to London and see other people and find some way out – there must be a way.[64]

The Uhlmans could not have known that, as early as October 1939, Croft had, in fact, pleaded for mass internment, suggesting to the Home Office that all enemy aliens between seventeen and fifty-five years 'should be conscripted into labour corps under specially selected officers'.[65] By 1939, his daughter had already been married to a refugee for three years. A couple of days later, he wrote another letter in which he pressed the Home Office to monitor the Communist activities of 'alien refugees'. In both cases, the Home Secretary, Sir John Anderson, who was himself opposed to mass internment,[66] answered politely but stressed the fact that 'many among the refugees will be found to be friendly to this country'.[67] Croft, however, continued to address the Home Office on this matter and in August 1940, as the Government was making its first concessions towards its policy, he sent Anderson a memorandum on 'Friendly Aliens', in which he defended the internment policy. Croft was deeply suspicious of refugees' supposed political convictions: 'Are we quite sure that the love of their families is not a stronger tie than the love […] for England […]?',[68] arguing against their good will on the presumption that their love for their own country represented the stronger bond:

> But would anyone dare to say that if 60,000 British refugees from some temporary government of persecution in Great Britain taking refuge in a foreign land would, in like circumstances, desire

> to see their homes destroyed and Great Britain brought to utter defeat? The question had only to be asked to be answered in a vigorous negative.[69]

He also doubted the tribunals' assessments and claimed that 'some of these aliens even in the "persecuted" category have already been proved to sympathize with the enemy'.[70]

Croft's world view, which saw the British as a superior race, also led him to consider as unjust the internment of prominent members of the British Union of Fascists (BUF), which had commenced in May 1940. He thought it unfair that 'enemy aliens' should be interned, while members of the BUF, 'British citizens […] who may be whole-hearted in their desire for British victory',[71] were 'thrown into prison without evidence'[72] and were thus, in his view, treated in a worse manner than were 'enemy aliens'.[73]

In *The Internment of Aliens*, one of the first books on internment that was published as early as 1940, François Lafitte accorded Uhlman a full-page entry. Lafitte, who ardently criticized the policy of the Government, referred to Uhlman as a victim of the slowly decaying but still influential right-wing upper class.[74] He explicitly referred to Lord Croft's position in Parliament and to the fact that Croft's sister, Lady Edward Pearson, 'a well-known Blackshirt', had been detained by the police as a BUF member but released soon after. Although there is no evidence of Croft having intervened on behalf of his sister, his passivity towards his son-in-law's case remains striking. The historian Tony Kushner argues that ideological factors behind the internment policy, conditioned by the social and racial snobbery of the upper class, have not been sufficiently taken into account in research on internment, claiming that 'forces whose ideology was shaped by the world-view of clubland dictated government policy over "enemy aliens"'.[75] Uhlman's case exemplifies the fact that some of the die-hard supporters of mass internment, like Lord Croft, were often influenced by an antipathy towards Germans and/or Jews rather than by evidence of a serious threat posed to England by the refugees.

It is not known how Lord Croft reacted to Uhlman's release on 31 December 1940 (though he was probably glad for his daughter Diana to have her husband back after six months). However, as we have seen, his daughter's worries had not changed Lord Croft's attitude to the policy of internment or to refugees in general. The internment episode only further underlined the fact that the political and cultural divide between the English aristocrat and the German-Jewish refugee was and would remain unbridgeable.

NOTES

1. On Uhlman and his works painted in Tossa del Mar, see Anna Müller-Härlin, 'Fred Uhlman i la Guerra Civil Espanyola', in Gloria Bosch and Susanna Portell (eds), *Berlin, London, Paris, Tossa … La tranquil, litat perduda* (Girona: Fundació Caixa Girona, 2007), pp.175–9.
2. Fred Uhlman, 'Journal of a Painter' [JP], vol. III (c. 1974–75), unpublished typescript, British Library, ADD 74737, p.6.
3. JP, III, p.6.
4. Letter from Francis Uhlman to the author, 21 December 2002.
5. Letter from Diana Croft to Uhlman, 19 June 1936, included in JP, IV (1976–78).
6. 'I owe her my life and […] without her financial help my work would have been impossible.' JP, I, pp.105–6.
7. For example, both Diana's friend Betty Sackville-West, as well as Diana's cousin, Sir David Baird, acquired works by Uhlman (see exhibition catalogue 'Exposition Fred Uhlman', 16–30 January 1937, Galerie d'Art Le Niveau, Paris). At Uhlman's first solo exhibition in London at the Zwemmer Gallery in November 1938, Betty Sackville-West's cousin, the author Edward Sackville-West, bought a painting, as did an aunt of Diana, Lady Brocket. See 'Statement of Account re the Exhibition of Your Pictures', Letter from Zwemmer Gallery to Uhlman, 16 August 1938, Uhlman Estate [UE].
8. On Michael Croft see Anna Müller-Härlin, 'Rebellious and supportive: the collector Michael Croft and artists in exile in Great Britain', in Andrew Chandler, Katarzyna Stoklosa and Jutta Vinzent (eds), *Exile and Patronage* (Münster: LIT Verlag, 2007), pp.45–54.
9. Diana Uhlman, *Croft Castle*, n.pl.: The National Trust, 2000 (first published in 1979). Diana Uhlman outlined her complete family history in this booklet. See also O.G.S. Croft, *The House of Croft of Croft Castle* (Hereford: E.J. Thurston, 1949).
10. *Who Was Who*, IV, 1941–50 (London: A.& C. Black, 1967), p.267.
11. Larry L. Witherell, *Rebel on the Right: Henry Page Croft and the Crisis of British Conservatism, 1903–1914* (Newark, DE: University of Delaware Press, 1997).
12. Ewen Green, 'Introduction', in Henry Page Croft, *The Path of Empire* (London: Routledge/Thoemmes, 1998) (first published in 1912).
13. Anon., 'Lady Ullmann [*sic*] geb. Page-Croft', in *Stuttgarter Nachrichten*, 26 February 1937: 'Die kolonialpolitischen Extratouren des sehr ehrenwerten Sir Henry Page Croft gegen Deutschland haben ihre natürliche Erklärung gefunden.'
14. This information has been mainly gathered from Witherell, *Rebel on the Right*, Introduction.
15. Telephone conversation with Rosemary (Posy) Poole, 28 May 2002.
16. Ibid.
17. Diana won the Prix Maréchal Foch, awarded to the best student amongst all the participating schools in England (letter from Caroline Compton, 16 August 2006). She attended the finishing school in Paris of a Mlle Fontaine and in Florence of a Mrs Lestrange. In addition to French, she also spoke Italian, Spanish, German and some Portuguese.
18. Conversation with Caroline Compton, Hampstead, May 2002.
19. Telephone conversation with Rosemary Poole.
20. Letter from Francis Uhlman to the author.
21. Letter from Diana Croft to Uhlman, 19 June 1936, UE.
22. Telephone conversation with Rosemary Poole.
23. Elizabeth (Betty) Sackville-West, later Barlow, was a cousin of Vita Sackville-West. See David Cannadine, *Aspects of Aristocracy* (London: Penguin, 1994), p.283.
24. Telephone conversation with Rosemary Poole; letter from Francis Uhlman to the author.

25. Recorded conversation with Francis Uhlman, Hampstead, 13 February 2000.
26. Diana and Betty's adventurous tour to Spain is not unlike the one taken by Jessica Mitford, another upper-class rebel who, aged 19, had eloped with her cousin to Spain during the Civil War period. While one sister (Unity) was an admirer of Hitler and another (Diana) was married to Oswald Mosley, founder of the British Union of Fascists, Jessica represented the radical left in her family. See Jessica Mitford, *Hons and Rebels* (London: Indigo, 1996).
27. Letter from Caroline Compton to the author, 24 September 2006. Diana's work for the AIA has so far not been given the credit it deserves; in two existing studies, which examine the AIA in some depth, her contribution to the organization is almost entirely ignored. See Robert Radford and Linda Morris, *The Story of the AIA* (Oxford: Oxford Museum of Art, 1983), and Robert Radford, *Art for a Purpose: The Artists' International Association, 1933–1953* (Winchester: Winchester School of Art Press, 1987).
28. Appeal, Croft Castle, Herefordshire, 1955: 'All forms should be returned to Croft Castle Endowment Fund, 47 Downshire Hill, London, NW3.'
29. Recorded conversation with Francis Uhlman.
30. Fred Uhlman, *The Making of an Englishman* (London: Gollancz, 1960), p.209.
31. Ibid., p.208. Uhlman stated that once a year, on Christmas Eve, Croft paid his grandchildren a visit.
32. W.L. Guttsman, *The British Political Elite* (London: MacGibbon & Kee, 1965), p.303.
33. Henry Page Croft, *Twenty-Two Months under Fire* (London: John Murray, 1917), p.xiii. Croft served in the army from 1914–16.
34. For detailed information see Panikos Panayi, 'The British Empire Union in the First World War', in Tony Kushner and Kenneth Lunn (eds), *The Politics of Marginality: Race, the Radical Right and Minorities in Twentieth-Century Britain* (London: Frank Cass, 1990), pp.113 ff.
35. Chris Wrigley, '"In the excess of their patriotism": The National Party and threats of subversion', in Chris Wrigley (ed.), *Warfare, Diplomacy and Politics* (London: Hamish Hamilton, 1986), p.102.
36. Ibid., p.103.
37. Lord Croft in the *Morning Post*, 1919, as quoted in W.D. Rubinstein, 'Henry Page Croft and the National Party 1917–22', *Journal of Contemporary History*, 9, 1 (1974), p.143.
38. Lord Croft in the *Daily Graphic*, 13 August 1919, quoted in ibid., p.145.
39. Tony Kushner, 'Beyond the pale? British reactions to Nazi anti-Semitism', in Kushner and Lunn (eds), *The Politics of Marginality*, pp.145, 153. Kushner's essay provides an insight into anti-Semitism in Britain between 1933 and 1939.
40. Tony Kushner, *The Persistence of Prejudice: Anti-Semitism in British Society during the Second World War* (Manchester: Manchester University Press, 1989), p.79.
41. Letter from Churchill to Croft, 20 June 1945, Croft Papers [CRFT], Churchill Archives Centre [CA], Churchill College, Cambridge, CRFT 1/8, CH/108. Cited in Paul Addison, *The Road to 1945: British Politics and the Second World War* (London: Jonathan Cape, 1975), pp.165 ff.
42. Letter from Croft to Churchill, 25 June 1945, CRFT 1/8, CH/109, CA.
43. Henry Page Croft, *My Life of Strife* (London: Hutchinson, 1948), p.288.
44. Ironically, Lord Croft did not hesitate to support the *Anglo-German Review*, a British pro-Nazi organ which ardently supported the policy of appeasement. See Simon Haxey, *Tory MP* (London: Gollancz, 1939), p.206.
45. Richard Griffiths, *Fellow Travellers of the Right: British Enthusiasts for Nazi Germany, 1933–39* (Oxford: Oxford University Press, 1983), pp.232, 261.
46. Croft in *The Times*, 12 October 1936, as quoted in Griffiths, *Fellow Travellers*, p.232.
47. Croft, *My Life of Strife*, p.273.
48. Ibid., pp.273–6.
49. Croft in *The Times*, 23 February 1937, as quoted in Griffiths, *Fellow Travellers*, p.261.
50. Pierre Broué and Émile Témime, *Revolution und Krieg in Spanien* (Frankfurt am Main: Suhrkamp, 1982), p.552. The Catholic Church itself estimated that 411 incidents of this kind happened between February and July 1936.
51. Haxey, *Tory MP*, p.214.
52. Henry Page Croft, *The Massacre at Castellon and Desolation at Bielsa: The Evidence*, leaflet, published by Friends of National Spain, 1938.

53. Henry Page Croft, *The Truth at Last*, pamphlet, 1937.
54. Letter from Croft to Lord Halifax, 6 April 1938, CRFT 1/13, HA/13/1, CA.
55. Paul Preston, *A Concise History of the Spanish Civil War* (London: Fontana, 1996), p.100.
56. Letter from Lord Halifax to Croft, 27 April 1938, CRFT 1/13, HA/14/1, CA.
57. Letter from Lord Halifax to Croft, 21 February 1939, CRFT 1/13, HA/18/1, CA.
58. Croft, *My Life of Strife*, pp.273–6.
59. Henry Page Croft, 'Memorandum Friendly Aliens', CRFT 1/2, AN/3/2/1, CA.
60. Croft, typed draft, n.d. [late June 1940], (reproduced in full in this volume).
61. Letter from Osbert Peake, Home Office to Croft, 26 July 1940, (reproduced in full in this volume).
62. Letter draft from Uhlman to Croft, n.d. [early August 1940], (reproduced in full in this volume).
63. Uhlman, Internment Diary, 16 September 1940: 'In the afternoon a letter arrives from Lord Croft. My letter seems to have made an impression.' Uhlman also noted in his diary that he received a letter from both Croft and Peake on 3 October 1940. Neither seemed to contain any news, however. On 5 December, Uhlman wrote to Lord Croft again, but received no reply.
64. Letter from Diana Uhlman to Uhlman, n.d., (reproduced in full in this volume).
65. Letter Osbert Peake to Croft, 2 October 1939: 'You wrote to the Home Secretary on the 15th September suggesting that all alien refugees between the ages of 17 and 55 should be conscripted into labour corps under specially selected officers', CRFT 1/17, PE 1/1, CA.
66. Peter and Leni Gillman, *Collar the Lot!: How Britain Interned and Expelled its Wartime Refugees* (London: Quartet, 1980), p.64.
67. Letter from Peake to Croft, 2 October 1939, CRFT 1/17, PE 1/1, CA; letter from Sir John Anderson to Croft, 16 October 1939, CRFT 12, AN/1, CA: 'It is perhaps unnecessary for me to add the assurance that a very careful watch on Communist activities in this country is being kept by the responsible authorities.'
68. Croft, 'Memorandum Friendly Aliens'.
69. Ibid.
70. Ibid.
71. Ibid.
72. Letter from Croft to Viscount Caldecote, 26 July 1940, CRFT 1/6, CA/5/1, CA.
73. This was not the case; BUF members were often treated courteously. On BUF members and internment see Dave Renton, *Fascism, Anti-Fascism and Britain in the 1940s* (London: Macmillan, 2002), p.22.
74. François Lafitte, *The Internment of Aliens* (Harmondsworth: Penguin, 1940), pp.187, 81 (Uhlman was listed under 'culturally valuable men'). Lafitte's book was an outstanding contemporary attempt to analyze and criticize the Government's internment policy.
75. Tony Kushner, 'Clubland, Cricket Tests and Alien Internment', in Tony Kushner and David Cesarani (eds), *The Internment of Aliens in Twentieth-Century Britain* (London: Frank

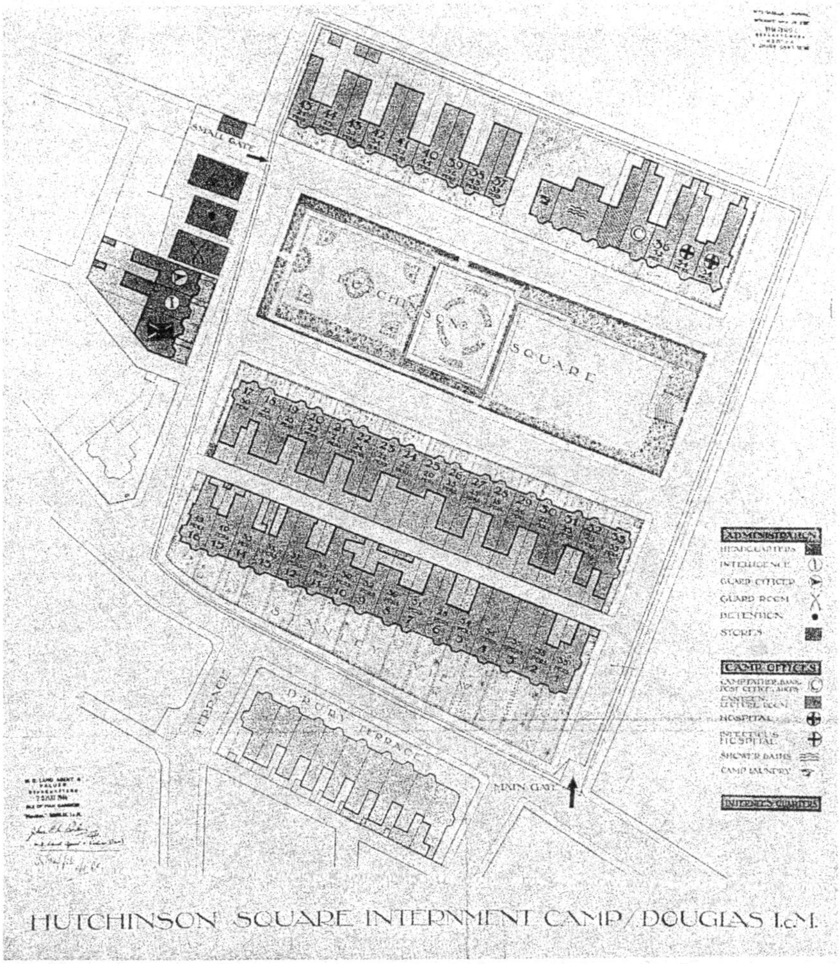

Figure 1. Map of Hutchinson Internment Camp, Douglas, Isle of Man. Reproduced by kind permission of Manx National Heritage.

CATALOGUE

2nd Art Exhibition
19.11.194o.
in Hutchinson Camp.

Please ask for Camp Prices.

FECHENBACH, Hermann.
3 Linocuts : "Internment"
"Released"
"Douglas"
4 Portraits
3 Oilpaintings : "Flower Stillife"
"View out of a Window"
"Back-Yards"

FLEISCHMANN, Peter
2 Portraits
Houses
Still Life

GUSSEFELD, H.G.
Decorated Tent Herrings

HAMANN, Paul.
2 Sketches for Life Size Garden Sculptures.
Portrait. (Donation for Home Office Auction.)

HELLER, Georg.
Portrait Sketches.

HENNING, Paul.
Linocuts : "Hutchinson Internment Camp"
The "To-and-From-The-World" Gate.
"Corner View"
"Camp Artist"
"Idyll"
"Almost Southern"
"Smiling Through"

HERTEL, Gerd.
Sketches on the German Anti-Nazi Fight
and the Spanish Fight for Liberty.

HOFBAUER, Frank.
"Boxes"

KAHN, Erich
Oilpainting : "Landscape"
"The Philosophers" (Monotype)
"Papageno and Papagena"
Carricature of Dr.Hinrichsen
and several Drawings.

KOHN, Johann.

Figure 2. Catalogue 2nd Art Exhibition, 19 November 1940, in Hutchinson Camp. Reproduced by kind permission of the IWM.

KRAEMER, Fritz.
Portrait of Dr.Fraenkel
Several Watercolours: Landscapes

MARKIEWIC, Herbert.
1 Portrait (Oil)
6 Portraits (Chalk)

MUELLER-BLENSDORF, Ernst.

A) Drawings: "Kneeling Woman" "Norwegian Fishermen" "Young Couple" "Lovers" "Nude Girl" "Girl with Hat" "Girl Arranging Her Hair"

B) Plaques: "Girl with Veil" (Mahagony) "Lady With Hat" (Stained Wood) "Lovers" Mahagony)

C) Sculptures:
Group:"Fugitives" (clay,cast in plaster)
Group:"Refugee Family"(" " " ")
Nude Girl (" " " ")
Fugitive Children (" " " ")
Figure of a woman (" " " ")
Relief "Adam and Eva" (" " " ")

PLANER, Felix.
Oil-paintings: Portrait of a Peasant; Study of Prees Heath Camp Life.

SCHREINER, Johann.	Architectural Designs.
SCHITTERS, Kurt.	Oil paintings: PORTRAITS.
SINGER, Dr.Erich.	Cartoons (Portraits and Carricatures).
SOLOMONSKY, Fred.	Portrait - drawings.
SONTAG, Mark.	Stage prospect to "Punch and Judy"
TECHNICAL SCHOOL.	Selection of technical instruments.
UHLMANN, Fred.	Oil paintings: "Douglas", "Ascot", "View of Douglas". Pen-, Pencil - and coloured drawings.
WIESSENBORN, Helmuth.	3 large woodcuts: Warth Mill, Douglas I and Douglas II. 9 woodcuts of medium size: 1 - 8: Stillife in the Camp. (first pages of a picture book) 9: Sitting man. 6 small wood engravings.

Price of catalogue: 2d

For prices of the works exhibited kindly ask attendants - Place your order for your portrait!

The vignette of this catalogue is an original work by Erich Kahn.

HUTCHINSON CAMP
DOUGLAS, I.o.M.

Figure 3. Catalogue 2nd Art Exhibition, 19 November 1940, in Hutchinson Camp. Reproduced by kind permission of the IWM.

REFUGEES

SIR,—The undersigned artists, painters and sculptors, at present interned in Hutchinson Camp, Douglas, I.O.M., would like to appeal urgently to all our British colleagues and friends. It is only too well known that we have left our homes and our countries as our persons as well as our work were greatly endangered there. We came to England because we believed that here we would find that liberty again which we had lost, and because we saw in her the last bulwark, the last hope of Democracy in Europe.

Instead of this we, whose only wish was to join all our efforts to hers, have been placed behind barbed wire. We were taken from our studios, and we are now here for an indefinite period of time. It is largely a matter of indifference to us whether we must submit to hardships in a greater or lesser degree—but we do not want to lose contact with the world outside. We want to create something that lives, something that perhaps, beyond the bounds of war, could be of the greatest use to this country. This has always been the mission of Art. Art cannot live behind barbed wire—whatever attractive pictures of life in an Internment Camp may have been painted by some newspapers. The tension under which we live here, the feeling that a great injustice has been done to us, the restlessness created by living in such close community with thousands of persons, the situation in which our wives and children are, from whom we have had no news for weeks, and the uncertainty as to the fate of works begun by us, which may since have been put into some cellar to moulder there, prevent all work and creative thought.

We ask our British colleagues and friends and all those interested in Art to help us. Please see that we have a fair chance for release. The "White Paper" makes provision for all sorts of classes—agriculturists and food producers, dentists and scientists—only the artists have, as is so often the case, been forgotten. Apparently we are not needed.

Please bring your influence to bear on the Advisory Committee and restore to us—all refugees from Nazi oppression—the one thing no artist can live and work without: FREEDOM.

E. Müller Blensdorf, Kurt Schwitters, Ernst Schwitters, Siegle Charoux, Paul Hamann, Fritz Kraemer, Hermann Rössler, C. Felkel, Fred Uhlman, Erith Kahn, Hubert Markievicz, F. Salomonski, Eric E. Sterz, Scory Ehrlich, Hellmuth Weisserbonn, H. Felhenbach, Fritz Krämer.

Figure 4. Artists' letter to the *New Statesman and Nation,* 17 August 1940. Reproduced by kind permission of the *New Statesman,* © 'all rights reserved'.

Hutchinson Camp, Douglas, I.O.M. House: 6..

CULTURAL DEPARTMENT.

Program Nr.17 11th.-17th.November 194o.

Day	Time	Speaker / Event	Subject	Place
Mon. 11.11.	11.oo	Prof.Jacob	Main Lines of World History (ctd)	H.41.
	7.45	Cercle Français		H. 5.
	8.oo	Rabbi Dr.Weiss	Fundaments of Jewish Thoughts I.	H.21.
Tues. 12.11.	4 .oo	Mr.W.Cohen	English Cercle	H. 8.
	7.3o	Pastor Kramm	The Conflict between German Protestantism and Neo-Paganism. I.	H. 1.
	7.45	Dr.Renner	Elements of Psychology	H.24.
	7.45	Recital	Shakespeare Sonette and Mr.Furth plays J.S.Bach.	H.14.
	8.oo	Prof.Marx	What is "Bildung"?	H. 3.
Wedn. 13.11.	4.oo	ART-EXHIBITION	Introductional talk by Dr.K.E.Hinrichsen	Hall.
	8.oo	Mr.Loewenberg	Impressions from a modern English-School.	H.13.
	8.oo	"Punch and Judy"	Kasperle-Theater	H.23.
	8.oo	Mr.Wittelshöfer	Reminiscences from German Postwar Ministeries.	H. 2.
Thurs. 14.11.	11.oo	Prof.Jacob	Main Lines of World History (ctd)	H.41.
	4.oo	ART-EXHIBITION	Introductional talk by Mr.Oppenheimer.	Hall.
	7.45	Mr.Freund-Corvin	Reading from own writings	H.28.
	8.oo	Concert	See Special Program (Mr.K.Wagener)	Hall.
	8.oo	Mr.Fiedler	Collective Experiences from another Camp.	Sm.H.
	8.oo	Rabbi Dr.Weiss	Fundaments of Jewish Thoughts II.	H.21.
Fri. 15.11.	4 .oo	Mr.W.Cohen	English Cercle	H. 8.
	3.45	Mr.F.Weiss	Film Directions	H. 5.
	7.45	Dr.Rosenberg	disraeli	H.27.
	8.oo	Debating-Society	See Special Program.	Hall.
	8.oo	Mr.Henning	Study-Group on Photography	H.36.
Sat. 16.11.	8.oo	Dr.Rusche	Problems of Criminology: Fate of some Criminals.	H. 1.
	8.oo	Dr.Friedenthal	Shakespeare and his Time III.	H.41.
Sun. 17.11.	3.oo	Youth-Group	See Special Program.	Hall.
	5.3o	Dr.Singer	The Fight against German Propaganda. III.	Sm.H.
	8.oo	Concert	See Special Program.	Hall.

Meetings of all CULTURAL WARDENS take place every Tuesday and Friday in the Hall at 9.3o a.m.

Douglas, November 1oth.194o.

Figure 5. Lecture Programme no. 17, Cultural Department, Hutchinson Camp, 1940. Reproduced by kind permission of the IWM.

ART EXHIBITION

To summarize the impression after visiting the Camp's Art Exhibition: It is astounding and encouraging to see how the artists under the given conditions did not loose heart. Each of them proved himself stronger than his accidental fate. The Quality of the exhibited works is generally good, partly excellent The variety of subjects choosen, the differency in apprehension and performance is most interesting and attractive.

Kurt Schwitters oil paintings show his well known mastery of the subject, enriched by a fine psychological accentuation in the portraits. The very contrasting technic of H. Fechenbach reaches the same effect with quite different means, slightly endangered by becoming sophisticated. This danger is avoided by H. Markiewitz whose coloured drawings, very light, full of living effects, are nevertheless more conventional than they may appear at first. F.Kraemer, on the other hand, follows a very definite style in his paintings, the dryness and coolness of which make it diffi cult for many laymen to appreciate. Fred Salomonsky's drawings are good illustrations of a keen eye and a nervous hand. Most refined and virtously done are R. Hirschhau - ser's drawings; and good taste as well as fine workmanship mark H. Weissenborn's woodcuts. Light, with the experienced technic of the stage-painter, are E.Stern's drawings. E. Kahn represents a more highbrowed type in his interesting exhibits. The same applies even more to F. Uhlmann. He chooses stranger abjects and the darker side of life to show a very delicate mastery of light-and shadoweffects. One can be sure that his artistic personality will secure him his own place without infringing on other artists of a similar kind.

About the sculptors who, unfortunately, could only show Photos of their works with a few exceptions- we should like to refer in our next issue, owing to lack of space in this one.

As the Commander remarks, we expect as soon as possible a second exhibition after this most promising start.

A.Z.

CHARADE

rus - et - bow - swal - er - cyp
ine - born - low - els - yes - in
rich - ter - nic - hol - rel - pok
guest - umb- ost - day - la.

1.) Mediterranean island
2.) Part of Lon don
3.) Part of court-trial
4.) Poison with most adepts
5.) Mr. Chamberlain's attribute
6.) Card game
7.) Intestines
8.) Tall bird
9.) The past 24 hours
10.) Little bird

The first letters, read downwards give an up to date slogan for everybody.

o

Third Party
- - - - - -

Mischa Elman and Jascha Heifetz were lunching together. The waiter handed Mr. Heifetz a letter simply adressed: " To the World's Greatest Violinist." " This must be for you, Mischa," Heifetz said, passing the letter. Elman, looking at the adress, shook his head. " No, it's yours, Jascha." Whereupon they decided to have the waiter read it. He opened it and began: " Dear Fritz -"

(Esquire, Chikago)

High Finance
- - - - - - - -

"Young man who gets paid on Monday and is broke by Wednesday would like to exchange small lo ans with a young man who gets paid on Wednesday and is broke by Monday."

(Advertisment in a New York paper)

Whatever becomes of the small neutral statesman who says:"Don't look now, but I think somebody is getting away with our country?"

(Detroit News)

Figure 6. 'Art Exhibition', review of the First Art Exhibition in Hutchinson Camp, *The Camp*, no. 1, 21 September 1940.
Reproduced by kind permission of the IWM.

2a   №10

The Camp

SUNDAY, NOVEMBER 24, 1940

EDITOR: M. CORVIN
PUBLISHED IN HUTCHINSON CAMP, DOUGLAS, I.o.M. ADM.: W.G. FEUCHTWANG

THE CAMPFATHER'S ADDRESS TO THE COMMANDER ON OCCASION OF THE OPENING OF THE SECOND ART EXHIBITION

Gentlemen:-

I am speaking for all the exhibitors and for the management of this occasion as well as for the entire Camp and I shall have the honour to ask our Commander to open this Art Exhibition which is the second of its kind. Before I do so let me say a few words on our behalf:

In the first place we wish to thank you, Sir, for the understanding help you have given us during these last four months. For many of us it is exactly 20 weeks today that we have been interned. This really friendly assistance has made it possible that the works which you find here could come into existence. The Artist, more than anybody else, suffers under the stress and strain of adverse circumstances. He might have stupendous and even divine inspirations - but he wants an atmosphere of kindness and friendliness around him shall that mysterious transmutation materialise: from thought and imagination into a work of art. Well, I hope that our artists have shown that they can work inspite of difficulties and a quite natural depression.

It is not said in vain that Love and nothing but Love is and can be the sole instigator, the only "momentum movens" of Art. And speaking of Love in the highest sense of the word: it is our Love for Great Britain that gives us the strength to be cheerful and hopeful inspite of our sad experiences. We know what is at stake, we know that Great Britain must be victorious shall humanity be victorious. All that counts is that Great Britain wins this war ...

That's why we want to help, to do our bit, as best every one of us can do, accoridng to his abilities, and in the right place.

We know, Sir, how interested you and your Officers are in our cases and that you do all in your power to help us to get our early release. We thank you, and your Officers, of all our hearts and would only ask you to carry on working ceaselessly for everyone in this Camp who can be released. And let's hope that there will soon arrive for us those good news for which we then shall be yet more thankful and, for which we keep on longing all the time.

So let me wind up this little speech by expressing my hope, that this will be a very successful exhibition, but our last one in internment.

And may I now be permitted to ask you, Sir, to kindly declare this exhibition, the Second Hutchinson Art Exhibition, open....

Figure 7. 'The Campfather's Address to the Commander on Occasion of the Opening of the Second Art Exhibition', *The Camp*, no.10, 24 November 1940.
Reproduced by kind permission of the IWM.

Figure 8. *Ascot*, 'Internment series', 1940.
Reproduced by kind permission of BM.

Figure 9. *Ascot – Two Figures Reading by the Fence,* 'Internment series', 1940.
Reproduced by kind permission of the IWM.

PART II

4. 'HM Loyal Internee': Fred Uhlman's Internment Diary, 1940

On 25 June, at 7.00 in the morning, someone knocked on my door. 'A gentleman wishes to speak to you,' said the maid. I dressed quickly and went downstairs. A policeman was sitting waiting in the dining room.

As I entered, he remained seated, playing with a pair of kid gloves. I asked him what he wanted. 'I'm sorry, but we have to intern you', he said. His voice was friendly, with no trace of reproach. 'Do you know my wife expects a baby in a few days?'[1] I asked. 'We know', he said.

I left him and went to my wife. She was sitting half dressed on the bed. 'I'll help you pack your case,' she said. We didn't say much; we had already spoken so often about this to one another.

'It's possible you won't hear from me for a long time,' I said.

'I know.'

'Will you perhaps go into hospital now? The baby can arrive any day and if there are air raids, the roads will be blocked.'

'I'll see, Darling.'

'Well, goodbye, and let's hope all goes well with our baby. Be brave.'

'Goodbye.'

We said goodbye. A large black limousine was waiting for me, the policeman closed the door behind me and took his seat beside the chauffeur. The car drove off slowly, my wife stood smiling in the doorway, I saw her dear, clear eyes one more time. Her rather deaf aunt,[2] who had understood nothing of what was going on, was leaning out of a window, calling 'Goodbye, Freddy! Good by-ee, Good by-ee!' in a warm, cheerful voice. Then the house, the trees and the flowers disappeared.

This is how I left Wareside to which I had only come a few days before from London, in order that my wife should not be on her own when her first baby arrived. The countryside that I loved so much was full of new life. We drove slowly through the country. It was a wonderfully fine summer's morning. I sat at the back of the limousine, in the front were a chauffeur and footman in dark livery. After driving for around twenty minutes through small villages we came to a housing estate, the car stopped in front of one of the awful, cheap, standardized houses, erected by some housing association or other, and the officer who had arrested me got out to arrest somebody else. After around twenty minutes he arrived back with an old man who sat himself next to me, his tiny suitcase on his knee. 'Professor Pollack,' he introduced himself to me. We started to talk and he told me that he was sixty-eight years old and formerly the headmaster of a Viennese grammar school. But, quite apart from that, he had had a particular interest in the history of the French Revolution and in the political literature of the 19th Century. We talked of Béranger's influence on German literature, of Herwegh, and then we were suddenly in front of the police station in Ware.

We sat down inside and waited for further arrivals. After an hour, several young Catholic priests appeared who had, I believe, been arrested at St Edmund's [College]. One of them asked if he could telephone Cardinal Hinsley and was permitted to do so. Then two further victims arrived. Herr Scheinemann and Herr ? [*sic*], both businessmen who had previously had a great deal of money. Herr Scheinemann immediately showed me the photos of his family. 'So a nice boy, mein Junge, so a nice boy und so clever,' he said. 'I really hope they won't want to intern him, what do you think, Herr Doktor? And he's so popular with the English, so popular.' Then he showed the policemen his photos and wept.

One of the policemen asked us if we wanted him to buy us anything. We gave him some money and he bought me some fruit and some chocolate. I would later be in great need of the latter. At one o'clock we set off for an unknown destination.

2.

I no longer know for exactly how long we drove. We came to a fairly large town called Watford and were led into a kind of gymnasium. As we entered we had to relinquish our matches. No one understood why. But we quickly learned not to ask questions. Clearly we were considered to be arsonists or suspicious characters. There were perhaps one hundred refugees sitting in the long dismal hall. Old ones and young ones. The young Catholic priests who had come with us from Ware sat somewhat apart. I tried to read a book but had to comfort Herr Scheinemann ('so a nice boy, mein Junge, so a nice boy and so clever'). Now I began to understand that all private life had come to an end, that it would be a long time before I could be on my own again; and suddenly and for the first time I felt depressed.[3] Up till that point it had been an interesting experience. After waiting for hours, we were loaded into lorries.

There were no seats. We sat down on the floor and made ourselves as comfortable as we could. We were about twenty men in a small narrow lorry, huddled up close to one another. No one knew anyone else. The youngest among us was around thirty, the oldest almost seventy. Armed motorcyclists drove ahead, to the side and behind our transport. After around half an hour the journey became almost unbearable. We were situated directly above the wheels, the suspension was poor and the air was filled with the exhaust fumes that penetrated the gaps between the boards. Several men had to vomit and the column was forced to stop on several occasions in order to allow the sick men to recover.

'And this is England?' said one. 'It's no different from the Nazis.'

'But gentlemen, we must be fair,' a man broke in, as he supported an older man's head in his lap. 'This has nothing to do with England. It's the fault of a few bureaucrats and half a dozen semi-fascists in the War Ministry and the Home Office. Not England! Wait and see. It's possible that it's just an accident, incompetence, a muddle. Wait till we get to our destination.'

Nobody else spoke. One and a half hours later we saw Windsor Castle in the distance and after a further half hour the convoy entered a small wood. We stopped. We had reached our destination.

3.

Before us there was a wall draped with barbed wire. Behind us were some huts. We entered and got ourselves into rows. Soldiers bearing fixed bayonets surrounded us. An officer delivered a brief speech, said something about discipline and good behaviour. Then he led us to our quarters.

Prisoner of War Camp 7, where we found ourselves, had once been the winter quarters of a circus. It consisted of several long narrow huts which were connected by a long corridor, a large hut and a lofty hall with a corrugated iron roof. This last had reportedly once been used to house elephants. One could still see the rings to which the wild animals had been tied. Now university professors were supposed to live there. Behind the huts there was a kind of wasteland that was surrounded by barbed wire and eight wooden buildings. A single tree in the midst of this vast dismal space served as a reminder that a wood had stood there not too long before which had since been cleared to create space for a firing range. The trees had been pulled out, roots and all.

The hollows still held the rain from the previous days. Sparse ferns grew between the craters, weeds bearing the palest flowers and a little grass. The ground was sandy and, when it grew hot, the air was filled with dust. There was no shade. Only a group of trees by the exit of one of the huts and a little summerhouse with room for two people to sit down afforded any shade. Round about there ran a wall covered in barbed wire which could be electrified. Machine guns were mounted on two of the wooden buildings.

First of all we were allocated to the various huts. I was sent to B Hut with around eighty to ninety of my fellow prisoners.

Let me now describe the hut in which I was accommodated. Upon entering, the first thing we saw was a urinal and a lavatory, separated from the dormitory only by a fairly low wall. Then came the dormitory, a long hall containing 90 wooden bunks. In each, three men slept above and three below one another. At the end of the hall was the washroom which, in contrast to the lavatories, could be closed off by a door. Apart from the wooden bunks, there were two long tables down the middle and a few chairs. We were given straw with which to fill our mattresses and two woollen blankets. In the meantime it had grown late and was getting dark. We were given bread and some tea. That was all we had received since

7 o'clock that morning. Then the electric lights were switched off. By the light of a single candle a few young rabbis were praying. Their heads, covered in prayer shawls, cast mysterious shadows. Then this light, too, was extinguished and night descended like a black owl on its fearful prey.

I was unable to sleep. The unaccustomed camp and the unaccustomed noises. The breathing of men en masse. The gurgling and snoring and whistling and grunting. The giggling of those who were unable to sleep when someone snored too loudly. The stench from the lavatories.

I know it's nothing special. Nothing that hasn't occurred a thousand times before. And yet a sensitive person will continue to experience it as torture, horror, humiliation. In this case it was perhaps made worse by the fact that sixteen and seventy year olds were lumped in together. The old men could not sleep, tried to find the lavatories in the dark, bumped into others, tossed restlessly on their hard beds and waited impatiently for the break of day. I myself only fell asleep towards morning. I loathed the camp and I loathed the people with their unfamiliar faces, their strange sounds and their smells. At home I had [...][4]

7 September 1940

Rawicz[5] plays ('Smoke gets in your eyes').

Frightful depression (Halifax speech[6]). I must master it. Must. Must. Schwitters[7] recites poetry. Rawicz: 'You are mistaken if you believe you will now be released.'

At night, in the next-door house, a fit of madness: 'There's someone at the door, they've come to kill me. I'm frightened, I'm frightened.' Then I hear: 'Sleep. Don't be afraid.'

Child: I love MAN. [...]

8 September

From a conversation: What's the date today. At least the 8th.

In the morning: deep depression. Can't eat anything. In the afternoon: Talk to Matuschka,[8] Jacobsthal,[9] Ehrlich.[10] (Däubler), marvellous nude drawing. Rumours of several air raids on London. William Cohn:[11] China-Japan [...]

9 September

The same depression again. Fight against it. Desperate. But neither courage, nor logic nor reason can help. Strange sickness of the soul. Permanently afraid of not being able to cope mentally. Too much tension. Constant ups and downs. Reluctance to see other people. Claustrophobia.

In the evening, lecture by Cohn. India (Buddhism has disappeared. Now only in Ceylon, Cambodia, Siam, Japan, China.) In the afternoon, rather too clever lecture by Pater Aihinger[?] about Hinduism. Tomorrow will try to get myself a studio.

10 September

Today considerably calmer (despite the bad news from London).[12] Depression doesn't set in until the evening.

Three works: (Death with a child on his shoulders; Christ among skulls; 'Stuck fast').

In the afternoon, lecture on graphology (two things that can't be determined from handwriting: age, sex).

In the evening, Ehrlich. (Form is everything. Egg. The ear as a mussel.)

11 September

Best day for weeks. Am calm, almost cheerful. (How come? Periodic restlessness?)

In the morning a drawing ('Too late'). Receive permission to use Hamann's[13] studio. Sit for Schwitters. Astonishing interpretation of my face as a 'mask' (complexity, changes of expression). In the evening excellent lecture by William Cohn: The Japanese interior (i.e., that of a collector). Buddhism takes over the Hindu Gods as servants of Shintoism in Japan. The Kaiser as 'Führer'. Indian sculpture strongly erotic. Many breasts. In Buddhism that completely disappears. Sometimes one hardly knows if it is a woman or a man. Comes from Gandara (Hellenistic influence. Alexander the Great). India: devoid of charm, place, history. All mythology.

12 September

Quite a good day. In the morning a drawing: 'Last resort.' In the afternoon, my own lecture.

(The dentist musn't touch any of my teeth, he immediately wants to pull them out.)

In the evening, poems by Matuschka.

13 September
Calm, balanced. Schwitters tells stories (how the bedbugs got into the Academy, the black 'glass', the mushrooms [...])

14 September
Most cheerful day since my internment. Exhibition (Ehrlich, Krämer,[14] Fechenbach,[15] Markiewicz, Kahn,[16] Hirschenhauser, Blensdorf,[17] Hamann. Touching. Ehrlich in his corner. Beer afterwards! Rawicz plays 'To Freedom'. In the evening: meeting in the hall. Schwitters very amusing. Young man with 'Britain' sweater. Olympic Games.[18]

15 September
Continuation of the exhibition. Enormously popular. Captain Jurgensen.[19] In the evening Cohn: the Japanese squat on the floor, paint in the same position, the Chinese sit on chairs. In landscape, no plains, but always mountains and water. Almost always the same traditional eight landscapes. Never from nature. Pictures are painted at home from memory and from impression. Huge importance of the material (paper, hundreds of types of paintbrush, countless different inks, mounting of picture).

16 September
Frightful weather (what will it be like in a few weeks' time? Not to speak of the winter). Fluctuating moods. Fed up with many of the faces again. In the afternoon a letter arrives from Lord Croft. My letter seems to have made an impression. In the evening William Cohn: India.

Little known about history. For ages we only knew about the time up to the 3rd century. Important excavations two decades ago.

'Indus Culture' (3rd millenium). Relations with Mesapotamia? Script (cuneiform) not deciphered.

Iranians: Aryan in the middle of the second millennium.

Alexander (Gandara: Graeco-Buddhist culture).

Scythians – Huns.

Mohammedans (Mongol dynasty until 19th Century).

English.

Height of the flowering of Indian culture 400–700 (Tang 700). Art almost entirely religious. It's necessary to put aside, to forget all thoughts of European art.

Architecture: sculptural. Spatial considerations are of secondary importance. Often only a tiny cell in a religious monument.

Relief sculpture.

17 September
End of the exhibition. Prof. Cohn released. What a loss for us. (Prof. Heinemann,[20] Misch,[21] Goldmann,[22] Rothfels,[23] Mendelssohn-Bartholdy [are still here]). Letter to Sir Robert Witt.[24] In the evening: Schwitters. Mood bearable. Tomorrow two hundred new arrivals. ('Show me your left hand.' 'You will hear from me tomorrow.') Two or three illiterate men in the camp. (Cohn's address: TOOT BALDEN, OXFORD.)

18 September
Relatively calm. Bad news from London. The Commandant[25] has a coat of arms made HUTCHINSON I CAMP = 'Happiness' in Cooperation! Works: 1 picture, 2 drawings. […] with new arrivals. Conversation with Arnoldi.[26] (Why is the child so alone? Without its father or mother?)

19 September
Calm day. Depressive intervals. Letter from Diana. Otherwise nothing of importance.

20 September
Calm. One drawing […]. Receive Baudelaire! Receive Diana's telegram. Lecture by Unger.[27] Greek philosophy. In the evening, 'debate' Lenin[?]: portraits and portrait painters.

21 September
Calm. Fine clear day. Post: Diana, Jonny,[28] splendid letter from Francis.[29] In the evening, lecture by Friedenthal,[30] Cortez.

22 September
Calm day. One drawing. Leavetaking: Prof. Goldmann, Pfeiffer,[31] Kastner.[32] Visit Prof. Jacobsthal, Wellesz,[33] concert. *Magic Flute*, Chopin, Glas.[34] Leaving party Kastner, fantastic mood. 'Are you getting out today? Very good' (Eisler).[35]

23 September
One drawing. Two oil paintings finished. Lecture: Should the artist portray his age?

24 September
Olden dead![36] One drawing. Oil painting no. 3 started. Continuation of the discussion of yesterday evening. Violent attacks of colleagues. Unfortunately Ehrlich too. In the evening lecture on Cortez (Friedenthal). Thank God, calm since 11th September. Frequently rather depressed. But not so disturbing.

25 September
Interned three months ago today. How we took leave of one another, smiling! Diana's telegram. (Father wrote Home Office.)

Birthday celebration at Blensdorf's. Schwitters, Hamann, Krämer, Ehrlich, Franck and Franck.[37] Delightful. Astrology as self-gratification. 'Happiness in Cooperation'. 'Hospitality in concentration.' 'Happiness in constipation.' 'Haemorroid in consideration.' [...] Blue-white-red (blue = blue pencil, white paper, red tape. In the evening, Rawicz; [...] Wellesz. Return to the classical theatre [...]

O.B.H.: Order of British Hospitality
Intern the lot – drum, drum, drum
Release the lot – drum, drum, drum
Intern, release
Intern the lot – drum, drum, drum
Release the lot – drum, drum, drum
Why not?

26 September
Nothing of importance. In the evening: Cortez (1st conquest of Mexico). (Bilbo alias Traven.[38]) 1 drawing.

27 September
Nothing of importance. Am anxious. Raid on London N.W.!? Wolf under arrest because he didn't declare a blanket.

28 September
Nothing of importance, Striking number of people with barber's itch, facial rashes (bromide? blankets?). Commandant is collecting

an album of art. So is the sergeant major. The animal tamer's window. Lathe. One drawing.

29 September
Rather nervous day (probably because of the large number of releases). Prof. Jacobsthal (Oxford, Christchurch?) is going.

In the evening, lecture Prof. Isaaks: history of therapy. One drawing (probably the conclusion to the 'ecclesia militans' cycle). What's going on in London? What are the people thinking there? Odd how far away we are. How strange! Time doesn't exist for us, we are just counted like cattle! (cf. Richard III in the Tower)

30 September
Letter to solicitor. Painting doesn't appeal to me at the moment. Pictures are inexpressive, without experience and freedom. Just want to draw. Lecture Franck, 'Seeds of modern architecture'. One drawing (scarecrow).

1 October
Bad day. Grey sky. Fear of winter. In the evening great discussion: 'Is there such a thing as non-political painting?'

2 October
Still nervous and agitated. Impatient. Two drawings (scarecrows lashed by the storm). In the evening: animal tamer Neunzer:[39] About animals: how one shoots the rattlesnake. Okapi […]

3 October
Baby three months old. Tiring birthday celebration. Twenty-five guests. Blensdorf's present. The wicked fairy Anderson goes. Morrison Home Secretary.[40] Letter from Lord Croft and Peake.[41] In the evening Cortez, final part. One drawing.

4 October
One drawing. Lecture about windows. Discussion on art: […] Rethel,[42] Friedenthal, Unger. In the evening Wellesz. Byzantine music […]

5 October
Schwitters' 'Silver Wedding'. Four studies. Lecture on Montaigne

(Pariser)[43] (*librairie*, [...], *mon père*, French language, *le paradis perdu*, Marquise de O.). Weather frightful.

6 October

Frightful weather. Conversation with Ehrlich. (About accepting everything from nature.) Artists the greatest scroungers and parasites, rooting around like pigs in rubbish in order to find pearls. Picasso,[44] Maillol are not ashamed to take the best from wherever they find it and to use it. Picasso says himself: I'm not an artist but a finder. How is it possible to build on from, to extend further, someone like Barlach, Lehmbruck (who were great artists). One does not have to add anything to a face, one must let it express itself, as it is. Goya did that. He didn't add, he reproduced and accepted what nature gave him. [...] (Pastor Crämer tells us of Prees Heath. The guards, the whole night: Number one all right, number two all well etc. Later, number one get up, number two to hell etc. The one-eyed Commandant of Warth Mill. Fathers and sons deliberately separated.)

7 October

Fine day. Aimless. Wedding. In the evening: Herr Wendriner.[45]

8 October

Frightful weather. Nothing to report. Two drawings. Herr Martin H. simulating.

9 October

Frightful weather. No-one released for days. Can't do anything but read. The last post from Diana is dated 23rd September. In the evening, Dr Zuntz[46] reads *The Odyssee*. '*Andra moi ennepe*' (I was badly affected) '*hos mala polla plagkhth?*' – 'and he who wanted once again to see the smoke of his native land ascend or die'. How close that is to us today!

Coffee conversation: Blensdorf, Ehrlich, Hamann, Krämer, Franck, Jakob, Wellesz, Pariser, Zuntz, Henning, Dr Sluczewski,[47] Kastner, Friedenthal, E. Kahn, Hinrichsen,[48] Dr Singer, Sohn-Rethel.

Experiences of a Berlin worker by the name of Hertl in a concentration camp, Spain, France, Dunkirk.

10 October

A few hours of sun. Pleasing letter from Artists' Refugee Committee

(Article 8).[49] Lecture Wellesz: music of the middle ages (wonderful music of the 9th–12th centuries that we are only now beginning to recognize. Oxford, Cambridge, monks in religious orders. That's how music became an academic subject). In the evening Friedenthal: America-England. England in the 18th century. (Lord North, Lord Germaine.) [...]: Swift, Defoe, Sterne, Goldsmith, Locke, Hume, Johnson etc., etc. On the one hand, dissipated, immoral England. On the other puritanical, narrow America. Afterwards: Rawicz plays. One drawing. Zuntz recites *The Odyssee*. Unfortunately a moon.[50]

11 October
Drawings for the Commander.

11 October [*sic*]
(Friday) Fine day but full of anxiety. Impatient. Terribly homesick for my wife. Two drawings (one for the Commander). Arbitration between Markiewicz and Hirschenhauser on account of expropriating blankets! (I demand my rights, I demand my rights, I demand my [...])

In the evening: Discussion with Pariser about Montaigne (influence on Rousseau, *Emile*, *Confessions*), affinity with Marcel Proust. Speaks about the impossibility of grasping a serious event. Proust calls it '*la défaillance du coeur*'. (Death of his beloved grandmother. Not until some months later is he reminded of it by a suitcase that he would use whenever he visited the old woman; only then does he fully realize his loss.) Montaigne mentions that as well: '*La moindre surcharge brisa la barrière de la patience.*' Montaigne says of himself: My attitude when I don't want to lose the thread of a conversation, is '*constraint, sec et reservé*'. Montaigne speaks of his absentmindedness: he forgets the password, even his name (*je suis si excellent en oubliance*). I can't distinguish between oats and barley, nor between cabbage and lettuce, don't know that bread is made with yeast. [...] Strange type, Pariser. Textile manufacturer who, for instance, is writing on the sociology of fashion. Start of Yom Kippur. Rabbi Weiss. Moonlight. [...] in the sky.

12 October
Wellesz, Ehrlich, Pariser released. Fine day. Some sketches – no desire to work. In the evening: Homer. Optimistic letter from Diana. Sleep very fitfully. Wake after a few hours. Wild dreams.

13 October
One drawing, several sketches (Ehrlich's brown ink!).[51] In the evening Zuntz: How the Bible reached us. Old well known texts. [...]

Moonlight. Afraid for London. How far away it is. A strange world. It's frightening. One we don't [...] and can't understand. I wonder what it looks like. How does one get home? Taxis? Telephone? How do I get out of London? How do I get home?

14 October
Two sketches. Bad toothache. Must finally have it out tomorrow. Awful. Anecdote about Jurgensen and the Jew. 'What's your wife's name?' 'Don't know.' 'But you must know your wife's name.' 'Don't know.' Are you married?' 'Yes.' 'So what's your wife called?' 'How should I know, she walked out on me 38 years ago!' To Jurgensen (calling after him): 'Hey, do you have a cigarette?' J. gives him 6*d*. and goes on. Calls after him once more: 'Hey! Cigarettes cost 7½*d*.' (Several illiterate men in the camp.) In the evening: Zuntz: Homer. Poker!

15 October
Nothing of importance. Terrible night (toothache). Tooth out. Miserable day. No post. In the evening, cabaret.

16 October
One drawing (sale). Rawicz released! In the evening Homer (finished the 1st book). Wonderful. What delicacy, balance, wisdom. Two examples of superstition. Extraction of tooth = overcoming of obstacles to release. The 16th = 4 x 4 (Diana's lucky number) etc. Scandal about the open letter in the Camp newspaper. Herr Warschauer[52] is looking for [...]. Denunciations. The Commander wants to destroy the typewriter.

17 October
One sketch. Rawicz farewell party. (Smoke gets in your eyes.) What will it be like in London? How will we behave when faced with this danger? What food is there bromide in? Discussion about informers. Article in *Tribune* about Lord C[roft].[53]

18 October
Pretty bad news. No release probably to be expected for a long time.

Feel very depressed. I so long for Diana. Went for a walk. Charming area. (An enchanting house, Pompey red.) Otherwise did nothing. Just read the history of Ghengis Khan. Interesting conversation with Friedenthal. He is correct in his assertion that there is an astonishing vitality here in this tiny microcosm. What energy. What fantastic experiences, e.g. lion tamer, Hertl, Müller-Blensdorf (4 years as a sailor, came back sick with the plague. 2,500 people were thrown overboard on the journey from Gibraltar to England at the end of the war). Lieutenant Cooper sings German songs.

19 October

Constant depression. Everything looks black. Will I ever get out? How much longer? Few releases this week. […] in London.

Start diary.[54] Bach concert (Furth[55] 18 years old). Last lecture of Friedenthal's, America-England. Terrible weather. Darkest night.

(Friedenthal: a man before a sailor, a sailor before a foreigner, a foreigner before a dog, a dog before a soldier.)

20 October

Particularly severe depression with feelings of disgust, tension, not able to work. Atrocious weather that contributes to the despair. Not able to see anyone. At midday lecture by Dr Wiener […]

In the evening improvement at Dr Fraenkel's[56] statement that the White Paper can be expected any day now.

21 October

Depression. Improves after receiving a letter from Witt and on the sun coming out. Not able to achieve anything, but have a few new ideas. (Oil painting impossible. Can't concentrate. No peace to experiment. […] Colours always too bright.) Radio: new White Paper. Severe disappointment for the camp. Eminent artists?[57]

Raid on Liverpool? […]

22 October

Wonderful October day. Walk. Enchanting view. Mood good. Sit the whole day in the sun (two sketches). Depressed again in the evening. Try again and again to be rational and pull myself together. By comparing, considering. Nothing helps. Am I so weak or do others suffer just as much? Am I more sensitive or weaker or madder? Am I more cowardly than others? Perhaps I have never suffered before.

Note on Genghis Khan: Mongols (not to be confused with Tartars) […] 1218–1227. The Mongols ruled in China until 1368, in India they remained until the middle of the 15th Century. 9 April 1241 Liegnitz (in Austria as far as Neustadt, on the Adriatic up to Ragusa). Retreat from Europe 1242.

23 October
Despite the bad weather, calmer than yesterday. Have more confidence. Nothing of importance. Two (bad) sketches. Read a little (*Pickwick*). Stories about Bilbo. Shameless […]

24 October
One sketch. Unpleasant surprise (eminent artists, outstanding). I hope I get on the list. Am filled with terrible restlessness. Can't think, can't act. Every attempt I make to go about things logically, calmly, fails. (With a break between 5 and 8 in the evening.) Then […] night. Palpitations. Nervous collapse.

25 October
Morning and afternoon very bad. Waiting constantly for post, for a miracle. All my efforts to fight against it fail. How will it go from here? Everything looks black. Improvement at 4 in the afternoon. Calm after all the destructive tension. Will go to Friedenthal's lecture tonight.

26 October
Am very much calmer. Can work again. Three sketches. Glorious day, full of beauty. Telegram. Home Office decided to submit my case to tribunal. Believe this is a real step forwards. Am for hours 'perfectly happy'. Also read with great pleasure Lin Yutong, *The Importance of Living*. In the evening, Zuntz: Homer. Speak to J. Marshall about the prehistoric Isle of Man, own parliament, laws, barristers etc. Going to the Museum tomorrow. (Reporter to and representative of the English Government.)[58]

27 October
Museum visit in the morning (prehistoric, Celtic grave […]) Visit Zuntz in the afternoon. Poker in the evening, mood fairly calm. Schwarzschild released.

28 October
Pleasant walk. Calm. One drawing, two poems. Very good evening of Homer.

29 October
Grey, cold day. Nothing of importance. Thinking, reading. One drawing, two poems. In the evening chez Blensdorf. Finish first reading of Lin Yutang, lasting impression.

How oft in chaos of the night
Far off the watchman's steps resounding
The gentle clink of bayonet
The dew from barbed wire fences falling.

How oft in icy winter storms
When loud the cold dead cedars groaned
The ravens harshly from tall towers
Would croak for mercy from their god.

I thought with rueful shame and grief
Of thousand flowers I'd failed to smell
Of lakes and birds still unadmired
Of final words I'd left unsaid.[59]

30 October
Grey day. Nothing of importance.

31 October
Grey day – but glorious evening. Dark red clouds, then whitish green – telegram from Diana: R[oyal[A[cademy] recommends release!?[60] I hope so. Nothing of importance. Learn a little linocutting. Am reading Duc du Lauzun, 'The Crusades'. Letters from Diana and Witt. What will November bring?

1 November
Kitchen duty. Nothing of importance. (Böhm three days in prison because he threw his fiancée some flowers.) Hamann small sculpture for the Co[mmander].

2 November

Concert (Handel, Bach, Mozart, Beethoven): Glas, Furth, Sluczewski. In the afternoon, Neunzer [...] lions, tigers, elephants: 50 years of experience. Never any friends. Constant danger. Black mamba (green mamba turns black, he claims). Wounds: tigers, lions, rhinoceros, anaconda snakes, wild elephants, leopards. Has treated everything himself. (Permanganate on the wound and a paste he made himself.) No scabs. No pus. Bites from scorpions, rattlesnakes. How to enter a lion's cage: the animal must prowl around, no whips or guns. Willpower and talking to the animal. A voice has a calming effect. (The lioness [...] from the table[?]. Rickety animal that's happy to be able to sit down.) Young lions are the most dangerous.

In the evening Friedenthal: Shakespeare and his time. Stage plays only serve a practical purpose, plagiarism is not seen as an issue.

3 November

In the morning conversation with Dr Streliska[61] (no beginning, no end). Life is there. Karma. Thousands of palm prints of people who have died violent deaths. Regarding mine: very versatile, hence no one outstanding talent. Delicate. Highly strung. hypersensitivity. Lungs? Slow metabolism. Business instincts (ancestors in business).

The light that heaven sent to me
And seagulls, goddesses in flight
And lilies blue on river bank
And thousand wonders were not yet enough
For me who for their meaning failed to ask.

Now that my fate has cast me into chains
(Not chains as such, but harsher, into fetters)
And bombs are falling round the silent plough
And cities filled with death and ashes still are burning
A single blossom would suffice
A thread from out the golden garment
That once I careless wore on shoulders bold.

4 November

(Married for four years.) Go 'mining' with Dr Bersu.[62] For manganese. Wonderful day and delightful landscape. Mountains rather in the mist just like in Grasse or in the Var valley. Amazing sunset,

St Patrick's Chair. Sketch a little, work a little.
Hirschenhauser gives me a sketch of Rudolf Olden.

5 November

Second consultation with Dr Streliska: abnormal sensitivity – strong tendency to melancholia (from my mother but also from my father's side), conscientiousness, inclined to pedantry – but mainly in order to create order – strong sense of self. Aesthete. As a painter, no 'intoxicating' colours. I don't luxuriate in colour. Architectural construction, aesthetic colouring. Criticism: too diverse. A plus point on the feminine side corresponding to a minus point on the masculine side. Thrifty (though this can be swiftly overpowered by a rush of emotion – for example, I go in a shop to buy one paint-brush and come out with ten).

Governed by powerful childhood impressions [...] Sadistic tendency as artistic impulse(!) Erotically inhibited. Commercial tendency (but strongly repressed). Cautious and reserved towards others. Exceptionally gifted. Biological longevity (but weaker in terms of vitality).

Several sketches. Letter from Diana.

6 November

Problems with the exhibition. Third conversation with Dr S. about Diana's writing: genuine humility – insecure towards others – therefore pride. No interest in company, society, dress. Hard to get her to act on her own account, only on behalf of others. Logical in retrospect (history?) but also acts on flashes of intuition that she later rationalizes – capable of sacrifice, open to influences (he didn't say easily influenced), vitality – sensitive but not hypersensitive – not imaginative – judicious – changeable in relation to others (friendly, critical, perhaps dismissive). Feminine. [...]

7 November

Very nice walk. Windmill, mountains, sunshine. Franck released! In the evening a concert (by invitation of the Commander), Glas, Furth.

Farewell party. Feel so bad. When, oh when?

8 November

A sad day. Zuntz is leaving. Farewell party. Letter from old Westheim.[63] Sent 2 July!

9 November

Try linocutting. I'm in a rather better mood. When I consider what a few months of internment amount to in comparison with what other people have to bear and have borne, I calm down again. Evidently the first Paragraph 19 cases[64] have also been released. In the afternoon: singing by Kurt Wagner (le musicien[?] de Marseille or 'the singing toad'). Charming! Neapolitan folksongs. Charming. In the evening Friedenthal. Excellent lecture. [...]

Speech by Capt. Davidson from Bloomsbury House.[65] Fantastic mixture of bribery and blackmail.

Now is the drear day over
The heavens empty, grey
The last sad fading flower
Sinks cold into the sea.

Why is my spring so distant
Why is my home so far?
I too would gladly follow
Through cold seas to times past.

Wherefore the noise, the calling?
The world is deaf and dumb.
The gods that we created
Now merely glittering dust.

Wherefore the ancient banners?
The new flags clatter bold.
And I, though I don't know it,
A lifeless spirit, dead.

Wherefore do we now suffer?
The victor grins and mocks.
And boasts of new times, ages,
Displays his mighty power.

And now a cloud arises
In heaven, empty, grey,
And star by star, processing,
Shine o'er the misty sea.

How is my winter distant
How is my home so near
How shall I now bid welcome
To what has come to pass?

10 November

GOOD day. Start a small sculpture with Hamann. Bold venture. Complete a poem. Also a linocut. Wagner again in the evening. Thoroughly enjoy myself. All in all a day without depression and full of work.

11 November

Continue work on my little sculpture. Stormy weather. Heavy rain. Mood very good (without knowing why, perhaps because I'm working again?!) Read *Robinson Crusoe* and make two small woodcuts. In the evening poker.

12 November

Nothing of importance. Further work on my sculpture. Sonnet by Shakespeare and music by Handel (flute).

Runkel moves in.[66] [...]

Good letter from Diana.

How long is it since trees were sprouting
And skies were blue, unscathed by snakes of fire?
When was it last that without fear, unfrightened,
Our ardent gazes met in one another?

When was it last that filled with longing
We spoke of wonders in far countries?
That we picked grapes ripe from the branches
Plucked fruit from off the laden fig tree?

When was it last that little children
Would scan the moon to find the man there,
Instead of frightened women's voices
That curse the bright light of the stars?

When shall we reach out to each other
And gain the treasure from each minute?

And when shall we begin our life
Anew, though lived ten thousandfold?

13 November

Work on my sculpture. Linocuts. One poem. Otherwise nothing of importance.

14 November

Three linocuts. Work on my sculpture. In the afternoon: ceremonial opening of our new café.

In the evening lecture by Rabbi Weiss. Release of Dr Unger.

15 November

Casting of sculpture. Case of Dr Arnoldi. Work: on religion (see appendix).[67]

16 November

Sculpture. One linocut. The case of Arnoldi (the secret comes out).[68] In the evening lecture by Friedenthal: Shakespeare [...]

17 November (Sunday)

Cleaning the floor as a punishment for arriving late at roll call. Two linocuts. Sculpture. Delightful evening in the café. Solomonski [69] singing, Furth playing.

18 November

When once in times that now are distant
Greeting the evening confidently
To blessed shore we'd quietly ramble
And speak of horror and of childhood fears
As when engulfed by dreams in lowering deepest darkness.

When once in times that now are distant
The clear sky radiant with divine confidence
Through open country hand in hand we'd ramble,
Then thought we of the horrors of long parting
And welcomed dreams and death and darknesses.

Work for the exhibition. Mood has been calmer in the last few days. Moments of complete peace. One linocut. I'm dissatisfied with the sculpture. Much too reminiscent of kitsch. Evening of Morgenstern.[70]

19 November
In the morning, 11 o'clock, opening of the exhibition. At 1.30 first visit to the cinema (600–700 men, virtually unguarded). In the evening a concert: Prof. Pollmann,[71] Furth, Sluczewski, Hamann (Schubert and Brahms Lieder, Bach sonata).
Exhibitors: Hamann, Uhlman, Blensdorf, Schwitters, Weissenborn,[72] Krämer, Solomonski, Kahn, Markiewicz, Fleischmann,[73] Fechenbach. Caricatures: Singer.[74] Commander seems very pleased.

20 November
Work – exhibition – 5.30 tiring party for Ahrends[75] (Furth and Heidegger [?] played Handel sonata for piano and recorder). An atmosphere such as I've only rarely experienced before.

21 November
New sculpture. Linocut. In the afternoon: performance by Sefton Camp (The Fairy Tale).[76] In the evening, lecture by Beran about education.

22 November
New sculpture – wonderful day (like a day in late autumn). In the afternoon, Capt. Jurgensen, case of A[rnoldi] and Thorn[?].
In the evening, café, poker. Release of Mehler, first case of Article 19, anti-Nazi. Letter from A[rtists'] R[efugee] C[ommittee] about R[oyal] A[cademy] recommendation. Curiously, remain calm the whole time.

23 November
Sculpture. Jurgensen interviews me concerning Bilbo. One linocut. Delightful evening: Glas (Chopin waltzes), Corvin[77] reads, Jacobi imitates Schwitters, recites Burck[?]. Schwitters recites 'The Piano' (absolutely excellent). Glas plays again. Present were Henning, little Fleischmann, Fraenkel, Beran, Hamann, Blensdorf, Corvin, Fürth, Glas, Sluczewski, Krämer, Solomonski, Hinrichsen, etc., etc. (Hamann tells me about his dream: he, Krämer and I had been released. At the same time he was told by one of his housemates, very agitatedly, that he had dreamed he had cut himself badly

while shaving and was bleeding heavily. A few minutes later a piece of the ceiling falls on his head. Unconscious. Bleeding.)

24 November
Nothing of importance. A little work. One drawing.

25 November
Interned for five months. (Why? Why?) Nothing of importance. In the hall I speak about Paris. One drawing.

26 November
Work on sculpture. Two drawings. In the evening, lecture by Ahrends.

27 November
End of the exhibition – one drawing – little party at Schreiner's. Radishes and beer. Schwitters's son[78] comes.

28 November
Sculpture – one drawing. Corvin reading. Arandora Star.[79] [...] Penguin Special, p. 187.[80]

29 November
Cast the sculpture. One drawing. Conversation with Peter Fleischmann. Poor devil. What can one do?[81] Guard steals Blensdorf's sculpture. Prohibition on visiting the cinema because of 'urination'. In the evening, at Kahn's.

30 November
Cut out the statue. Releases have virtually stopped over the last week. Everyone is tormenting himself with the question: will I at least be home for Christmas? In the evening, Friedenthal talks about Handel.

Sunday, 1 December
Depression. A little work. In the evening, *The Good Soldier Schwejk.*[82]

Monday, 2 December
Feel a little better. Two drawings. In the evening, a lecture by Sohn-Rethel concerning the development and source of National Socialism.

Tuesday, 3 December
One drawing. Mood more optimistic after [...] Morrison's speech[83] [...] Cinema. In the evening, visit Blensdorf. The baby is five months old.

Wednesday, 4 December
Nothing of importance. One drawing. In the evening, Beethoven Ninth.

Thursday, 5 December
Extremely anxious. Henning released. One drawing.
Letter to Lord C[roft]. Indignation about the new Sergeant Major, the blockhead. In contrast to Potterton.[84]

Friday, 6 December
Violent storm. Work very little. One drawing. Nervous. Am awaiting my release daily. Concert by Central Camp. Excellent string quartet. (Handel, recorder concerto, 'première' of Wellesz's [...]) Henning released.

Saturday, 7 December
One drawing (Thorn[?] released!!) In the afternoon a concert (Furth, Glas, Mozart sonata). Friedenthal on Haydn.

Sunday, 8 December
A little work but great anxiety. One drawing. In the evening, lecture by Dr Bersu: Isle of Man, 30 miles x 12 [...]

Monday, 9 December
Extreme anxiety. 'Release fever.' (Heavy raid on London.) Tiring birthday party. Sluczewski, Furth, Glas, Pollmann, Wagner. Slu [*sic*] talks about our 'common destiny'. Unimaginative. *C'est la musique qui fait le ton*. In the evening, Sohn-Rethel.

Tuesday, 10 December
And so another day has passed. Waiting, waiting. In the evening to a lecture on 'Expulsion of the Huguenots'.

Cinema. In the evening, poker.

Wednesday, 11 December
Another day gone. One drawing. Very depressed. Christmas!! Lecture on Huguenots.

Thursday, 12 December
Lecture by Fraenkel on Hollywood. One drawing.

Friday, 13 December
Nothing – waiting.

Saturday, 14 December
Waiting. Lecture by Friedenthal: History of photography. (Roger Bacon, Leonardo, Anastasius Kirchner: Laterna obscura, phantasmagoria, panorama, diorama etc.)

Sunday, 15 December
Waiting. (Glas, Schierer[?], Peltzer[?] released.)

Monday, 16 December
Farewell party for Glas.

Tuesday, 17 December
Appalling day. Waiting. (Fifteen people released, among them Unger, [...])

Wednesday, 18 December
Waiting – waiting. Can no longer work.

Thursday, 19 December–Monday, 23 December
Last few days were especially hard. The releases expected for Christmas failed to arrive. We few men who remained decided 'to try to make the best of it'. Not to talk about Christmas, but to be together and to try to bear it together and to hope for better things for the New Year. We will spend the evening of the 24th together as well as the 26th (about 20 people).

Completed four drawings.

Thursday, 26 December
Christmas passed. Bad, but yet [...] better then I had expected. Celebration on 24th and celebration on 26th. Losers of the

Hutchinson gang[?]. Our battle cry is shit three times over. (Weissenborn released.)

Sunday, 29 December

Am much too apathetic to continue writing. I go to bed every evening at nine. Sleep – anything so that I don't have to think. Everything disgusts me: the house, the food, the people. Now and then there are of course some good moments. A pleasant walk. The sun. A little hope. But in general everything is so desolate. I never knew that one's heart could ache so; and I never suspected how little consolation is afforded by the past, however pleasurable. The present is everything. Only today counts. Only freedom, freedom, freedom.

Finis

Afterword written in Bambers Green, Takely, Essex[85] in the presence of my beloved wife and child.

On 30 December, the day after I had despairingly written the word 'Finis', I received news of my release. I left the camp on 31 December. I arrived in London during the night of 31 December/1 January and contacted my wife. On 1 January I travelled to Bambers Green (a few days previously this part of Essex had ceased to be designated a 'protected area').[86]

NOTES

Transcribed, annotated and translated from the original handwritten German by the authors of this volume. Ms in possession of Imperial War Museum [DDF, IWM, 78/19/1]; original in Uhlman estate.

1. Although Uhlman had been in Britain since 1936, he was still not completely fluent in English in 1940. One reason for this was that in the first few years of their marriage he and Diana spoke mainly in German to one another.
2. Towards the end of her pregnancy, Diana was living in the country with her aunt, Mary Baird, in Wareside near Ware, Hertfordshire. Uhlman had only recently joined her there from London when he was interned.
3. Uhlman had in fact crossed out the words 'for the first time I felt depressed', but the words with which he replaced them are illegible.
4. Here and throughout, […] indicates missing or illegible word or words. Unfortunately Uhlman's diary entries from here until 7 September have been lost.
5. Maryan Rawicz (1898–1970), Polish pianist from Vienna (one of the celebrated duo Rawicz and Landauer), was interned while on a concert tour in England.
6. Lord Halifax was the Foreign Secretary. On 5 September he had declared in the House of

Lords that 'there will for a long time be many people – indeed there may be some until the end of the war – who are in fact devoted to our cause but who nevertheless are not let out and left at liberty'.

7. Kurt Schwitters (1887–1948), artist, leading Dadaist, emigrated from Hanover to Norway, arriving in Britain in 1940.
8. Count Franz Josef Matuschka, poet.
9. Paul Jacobsthal (1880–1957), professor of archaeology, emigrated from Marburg to Britain in 1935; one of a number of academics from Oxford University (others including William Cohn, Egon Wellesz and Günther Zuntz) interned in Hutchinson Camp.
10. Georg Ehrlich (1897–1966), sculptor, emigrated from Vienna to Britain in 1937.
11. William Cohn (1880–1961), art historian from Berlin, emigrated to Britain in 1938.
12. The bombing of London had started three days before, on 7 September 1940.
13. Paul Hamann (1891–1973), sculptor. Hamann emigrated from Hamburg to Britain in 1936. He was a good friend of Uhlman. In London, prior to their internment, Hamann and Uhlman were the main representatives of the Fine Arts Section of the Free German League of Culture.
14. Fritz Krämer (1905–), Austrian painter.
15. Hermann Fechenbach (1897–1986), painter, emigrated from Stuttgart to Britain in 1939.
16. Erich Kahn (1904–1980), painter, emigrated from Berlin to Britain in 1939.
17. Ernst Hermann Müller-Blensdorf (1896–1976), sculptor, emigrated from Wuppertal to Norway in 1933, arriving in Britain in 1940.
18. Uhlman recalled in *The Making of an Englishman* (London: Gollancz, 1960), p. 32, that this young man had been a member of the British Olympic team in Berlin in 1936.
19. The Camp's Intelligence Officer.
20. Fritz Heinemann (1889—1970), philosopher, emigrated from Frankfurt am Main via France to Britain in 1939.
21. Georg Misch (1878—1965), philosopher, emigrated from Göttingen to Britain in 1939.
22. Emil Goldmann (1872–1942), legal historian, emigrated from Vienna to Britain in 1938.
23. Hans Rothfels (1891–1974), historian, emigrated to Britain in 1939 (having previously spent two years as a visiting lecturer at Cambridge).
24. Sir Robert Witt (1872–1952), art historian and collector, who along with Samuel Courtauld and Lord Lee of Fareham was a co-founder of the Courtauld Institute of Art in London. Uhlman might have written to him in order to ask for a recommendation for release.
25. i.e. the Commander of Hutchinson Camp, Capt. (later Major) H.O. Daniel.
26. According to Uhlman's 1979 Internment Memoir, Arnoldi was 'our cook and almost certainly the only Nazi in our camp'.
27. Alfred Unger (1902–1989), writer, translator, emigrated from Berlin to Britain in 1937.
28. Jonny= John Heartfield (1891—1968), photomontage artist, emigrated from Berlin via Prague to Britain in 1938. Heartfield lived at the Uhlmans' home, 47 Downshire Hill, London NW3, from 1938 until 1943.
29. Francis= Francis Klingender, Marxist art historian, who also lived at 47 Downshire Hill for a while during the war.
30. Richard Friedenthal (1896–1979), literary scholar, writer, emigrated from Berlin to Britain in 1938; later, author of a roman à clef based on Hutchinson Camp, *Die Welt in der Nussschale* (Munich: Piper, 1956). Friedenthal and Uhlman kept in touch with one another after internment.
31. Probably Rudolf Pfeiffer (1889–1979), professor of classical philology, emigrated from Munich to Britain in 1937.
32. Rudolf Kastner (1879–), born Vienna, music critic in Berlin, said to have formed a chamber orchestra in Hutchinson Camp.
33. Egon Joseph Wellesz (1885–1974), composer and musicologist, emigrated from Vienna to Britain in 1938.
34. Richard Glas (1890–), pianist.
35. Robert Eisler (1882–1949), historian and economist, emigrated from Vienna to Britain in 1938.
36. Rudolf Olden (1885–1940), journalist and lawyer, emigrated from Berlin to Czechoslovakia in March 1933, then to France, and to England in November 1933 where he served as secretary for the German PEN Club in Exile. Olden and his wife drowned

in 1940 on their way to the United States when their ship, the *City of Benares*, was sunk.

37. One of the Francks, i.e. Carl Ludwig Franck (1904–1985), architect, emigrated from Berlin to England in 1937, was the man with whom Uhlman shared a room in Hutchinson. The other may have been the scientist B.L. Frank.
38 Jack Bilbo, pseudonym for Hugo Baruch (1907–1967), artist, art dealer, arrived in Britain from Berlin via France and Spain in 1936, opened the Modern Art Gallery in London in 1941; interned in Onchan Camp. One of a number of myths circulated by Bilbo himself concerning his identity was that he was the author B. Traven.
39. Herr Neunzer, also known as Brick or Blick, was one of Hutchinson's most colourful characters.
40. This comment refers to the replacement of the Home Secretary Sir John Anderson by Herbert Morrison.
41. Osbert Peake, Parliamentary Under-Secretary of State, Home Office.
42. Alfred Sohn-Rethel (1899–1990), economist and philosopher, emigrated via Switzerland and France to Britain in 1936.
43. Franz Pariser, textile manufacturer, with a great interest in literature and art.
44. It is not known why, in his 1979 Internment Memoir, Uhlman changed Picasso to Pissarro.
45. Character created by the writer Kurt Tucholsky.
46. Günther Zuntz (1902–1992), classicist, emigrated to Denmark in 1935 and to Britain in 1938.
47. Curt Sluczewski, lawyer and musician.
48. Klaus E. Hinrichsen (1912–2004), art historian, emigrated from Lübeck to England in 1939; at that time and since the chronicler of artistic activity in Hutchinson and other internment camps.
49. Apart from sending artists' materials to the interned artists, the Artists' Refugee Committee also played a role in the artists' release by vouching for them to the Royal Academy (who in turn reported to the Home Office). Diana Uhlman had been the Committee's secretary until she left London. Helen Roeder took over her role, but kept Diana well informed on the Committee's activities. Presumably Uhlman is referring here to the second White Paper of August 1940, *Civilian Internees of Enemy Nationality*, category 8 of which covered the release of 'scientists, research workers and persons of academic distinction'.
50. Reference to German bombing raids over Britain.
51. Ehrlich, who had been released the previous day, seems to have left his brown ink to Uhlman. Indeed, Uhlman did use brown ink in some of his internment drawings.
52 The 'Open Letter to the Commander' in *The Camp*, no. 4 (15 October 1940) made the case for allowing internees to work, and thereby contribute to the war effort, and suggested 'mica splitting' as a useful area. It is likely that the letter originated from Ludwig Max Warschauer (1898[?]–), an engineer and the founder of the Hutchinson Camp Technical School, where cleaving sheets of mica for use in the electrical industry was one of the skills practised. (On the mysterious Warschauer, see also Chapter Two, above.)
53. The article is almost certainly 'There has been treachery', *The Tribune*, no. 198, 11 October 1940, which refers to a 'great English gentleman in high office' with known Fascist sympathies.
54. This may refer to the first few pages of this diary (concerning his arrest in Ware, etc.), which Uhlman probably wrote down from memory at around this time.
55. H.G. Furth, pianist.
56. Heinrich Fraenkel (1897–1986), well-known journalist (*inter alia*, chess correspondent for the *New Statesman and Nation*) and author of anti-Nazi books, emigrated from Berlin to France in 1933 and then to England.
57. The third White Paper, *Civilian Internees of Enemy Nationality* (*revised*), that was published in October 1940, cited 'persons of eminent distinction' in art and other fields as a new category qualifying for release (see also, Chapter Two, above).
58. The reference is probably to a visit paid to the camp by Lord Lytton, Chairman of the Advisory Council on Aliens, which included among its duties the advice and assistance of the Home Office in the arrangements made for the welfare of internees.
59. Uhlman had wanted to become a 'poet or a playwright' when he left school (see *The*

Making of an Englishman, p.59). He wrote poetry as a student and lawyer, and continued to do so in his first few years of exile in Paris and London as well as during internment (when he noted the poems down in his diary). While Uhlman's internment poems are not among his best work, they are included here, as translated by the authors of this volume, as indicative of his moods and concerns at that time.

60. The Royal Academy had to write a letter of recommendation to the Home Office in support of the interned artists' 'eminence'. See also letter from Fred Uhlman to Diana Uhlman, 31 October 1940 (reproduced in Chapter Six, below).
61. One of several graphologists in Hutchinson Camp.
62. Gerhard Bersu (1889–1964), archaeologist, emigrated from Frankfurt am Main to England in 1937.
63. Paul Westheim (1886–1963), art critic. Uhlman and Westheim had met in exile in Paris where Westheim had supported Uhlman's early career. He emigrated from Berlin to Paris in 1933 and from France via Spain and Portugal to Mexico in late 1941.
64. Paragraph 19 of the White Paper permitted the release from internment of prominent anti-Nazis.
65. It is likely that the representative from Bloomsbury House (the London headquarters of the refugee welfare associations) made a speech encouraging the internees to join the Pioneer Corps, whereby they would also obtain their release.
66. After the architect Franck was released, Uhlman had to share with a new room-mate, Rolf Runkel. In his autobiography, he describes him as an ardent Communist without a sense of humour (*The Making of an Englishman*, p.242).
67. The appendix has been lost.
68. Presumably a reference to Arnoldi's National Socialist sympathies (on this, see also Uhlman's 1979 Internment Memoir).
69. Fred Solomonski, artist, singer and cantor.
70. Presumably the German author and poet, Christian Morgenstern (1871–1914).
71. Stefan Pollmann (1880–), singer, arrived in Britain from Vienna in 1939.
72. Hellmuth Weissenborn (1898–1982), painter and graphic artist, emigrated from Leipzig to England in 1939.
73. Peter Fleischmann, later Midgley (1923–1991), artist, came to England as an orphan and adopted the name 'Midgley' after the Manchester family who took him in.
74. Dr Erich Singer's cartoons were shown in the camp's second Art Exhibition.
75. Bruno Ahrends (1878–1948), architect, emigrated from Berlin to England in 1938. Played an important role in the camp's Cultural Department.
76. 'The Fairy Tale' was one of a series of scenes put on as children's entertainment by Sefton internees (see *The Sefton Review*, no. 2, 25 November 1940).
77. Michael Freund-Corvin (1897–), journalist from Berlin, editor of the Hutchinson paper, *The Camp*.
78. I.e. Ernst Schwitters-Guldahl, also interned in Hutchinson.
79. The *Arandora Star*, a ship carrying internees to Canada, had sunk on 2 July 1940 with great loss of life (Corvin was a survivor of the disaster).
80. Reference to F. Lafitte, *The Internment of Aliens* (Harmondsworth: Penguin, 1940), published in the Penguin Special series, on p. 187 of which Fred Uhlman and members of the Croft family are mentioned.
81. Presumably a reference to the fact that Fleischmann's official papers had gone missing, making it difficult for his case to be reviewed.
82. Play based on an unfinished novel by the Czech humorist, Jaroslav Hašek (complete with an up-to-date ending portraying Czech resistance to the Nazis).
83. Herbert Morrison had addressed the House of Commons on 26 November on official policy for releasing certain categories of internees from internment.
84. Sergeant-Major Potterton was a popular figure in the camp.
85. The Uhlmans had purchased a small cottage in Bambers Green, near Great Bardfield, Essex, where Diana went after giving birth to their daughter, Caroline. Diana and Fred remained there with their children – their son Francis was born in 1943 – until 1944.

5. *'The Story of Captivity': Fred Uhlman's Internment Memoir, 1979*

86. And was thereby no longer closed to 'enemy aliens'.

INTRODUCTION

I

So many millions have been 'liquidated' in this, the bloodiest century of all the bloody centuries in the history of man, that it might seem preposterous to speak about the 'sufferings' of some 20,000 enemy aliens who, compared with the horrors of the Gulag Archipelago, led a sheltered life in the fresh sea breezes of the Isle of Man, now a holiday resort for thousands of visitors and a haven for tax evaders. Of course this is true, I can reveal nothing worse than stories of muddle, stupidity and a few, very rare, cases of cruelty.

Why then do I want to tell the story of my internment if it was such a non-event in the middle of a most horrible war? My answer is that, however small, it is part of the English history of the war, that for me and almost all my friends it was not a trivial affair but a *traumatic* experience. The fact that millions suffered far more is no more relevant than to tell a man who lost one hand that others lost both arms and legs.

Believing this to be true, I feel justified to relate in some detail one of the most interesting experiences in my long life, a life so full of extraordinary events that I am inclined to believe that I had not one life but at least three.

Before relating the story of my internment it is unavoidable to tell in a few lines why I found myself behind barbed wire in Douglas, Isle of Man. To do this, I have to start at the beginning: the date and place of my birth. I was born on 19 January 1901 in Stuttgart, then the capital of the Kingdom of Württemberg, Germany's most liberal and in my opinion most civilized region. I became a Doctor of Law and a lawyer largely occupied in political cases (the defence of anti-Nazis), escaped to Paris in March 1933 after having been warned by the new Nazi Minister of Justice, Dr Dill, where, after having tried in vain to make a living as a journalist, art dealer, breeder of exotic fish, I started – successfully – to paint. Finding Paris, for reasons too long to explain, more and more intolerable, I went to Tossa del Mar, then an enchanting, unspoiled fishing village on the Costa Brava, just discovered by a few artists like Chagall and André Masson, where by the purest of all chances I met a young English girl who stayed there for a few days and left without leaving an address. (All this I have told in my autobiography *The Making of an Englishman*, London: Gollancz, 1960, a rotten title but a good book.)

When the revolution started I escaped from Spain, came to England and on 4 November 1936 was married in Chelsea Registry Office to the girl I had met in Tossa. From Chelsea we moved to Hampstead, 47 Downshire Hill, in 1938 where we are still living now. There I founded the 'Free German League of Culture', the only anti-Nazi cultural society in England at the time. Prior to that, I was involved with my wife and various friends in organizing an exhibition of German 'decadent' artists. I served as an A.R.P. warden after the outbreak of war and was interned on 25 June 1940 in spite of the fact that my wife expected any day the birth of our first child.

II

A few words about the Diary. Written 38 years ago, I found the largest part of it hidden under some drawings and I translated it from the original German into English. It was never intended for publication but as some kind of memorandum to remind me of events which I feared I would easily forget. As I wrote it only for myself, I used some kind of shorthand like 'Runkel' or 'Schwitters' or 'Jane Austen' which would make no sense to anybody but me. In such cases I told in some detail the meaning of these mysterious entries and I trust this makes the Diary far more readable.

— — — ooo0000ooo — — —

25 June 1940

On 25 June, 1940, at 7.00 a.m. a policeman came to see me and told me that he came to intern me.

'Do you know my wife is expecting a child any day and that I was here for one purpose alone: to be with her when the baby arrived?'

'I know,' he said.

I went to see my wife. She got up and helped me pack a small suitcase. She was calm as always in an emergency and very English!

'You may not hear from me for a long time,' I said.

'I know.'

'Wouldn't it be better to go to the hospital now? The baby might arrive any day and the wards may be closed during air-raids.'

'I will see, darling.'

'Well goodbye then,' I said trying to be very English too. 'And the best of luck.'

A big, black limousine waited for me. I got in and smiled at her. Her old aunt couldn't understand what was happening.

'Goodbye, Freddy,' she shouted. 'Bye bye.' She was certain that I was called away on an important mission. Perhaps the Government needed me?

And so I left Wareside. It was a wonderful summer's day. I passed a few small villages and the car stopped after some twenty minutes, when the policeman returned with an old gentleman who carried a suitcase.

'Allow me to introduce myself,' said the old gentleman. 'I am Professor Pollack, I have been headmaster of a grammar school in Vienna. I have been particularly interested in the history of the French Revolution and the poetry of the 19th Century.'

We talked about Béranger's influence on German literature, about Herwegh and at last stopped in Ware where we entered the police station. After an hour a few young Jesuit priests arrived and businessmen. One of them, Herr Scheinemann, showed me at once photos of his family. 'This is my wife,' he said, 'to the left my aunt Cicely, née Weil and on the right my brother Simon who is still in Germany. And this is my son. Such a nice boy, so clever. And so much liked by the English. I must show the photos to the police.' He showed them to one of the policemen and then started to cry. We left at 1.00 p.m.

and arrived at last in Watford where we entered a school. We had to surrender our matches (but why I have never discovered).

In the school were perhaps 100 refugees, old ones, young ones. I tried to read a book but I had to console Mr. Scheinemann who repeated endlessly, 'such a nice boy, such a nice boy and so clever'.

Now, for the first time, I realized that this was not a dream, that from now on I would have no more private life and for the first time I felt depressed and sorry for myself. Why should this happen to me of all people? Was I not a leading anti-Nazi who had fought against Hitler while the Cliveden set fraternized with him? Had I not warned again and again against Hitler? Had I not formed the only German anti-Nazi organization in England? Why, of all people, should *I* be interned? After waiting for hours and hours I was put in a lorry. There were fourteen seats and we sat on the floor; there were twenty of us. Some men were almost seventy, some younger. We sat crowded together, sitting over the wheels, tossed about and suffering badly from exhaust fumes. A few men began to vomit and the convoy stopped from time to time to allow the sick to recover. The man next to me shouted, 'If that's England why did I leave Germany? The Nazis were not better.'

'But, gentlemen,' said another, 'you must try to be fair. This has nothing to do with England. These were only a few bureaucrats. Perhaps this is only incompetence, muddle. You will see it will be much better once we have arrived.'

After two hours we did arrive!

— — —ooo0000ooo— — —

A small but dense wood entirely surrounded by barbed wire. We entered the camp and lined up. Before us were large wooden buildings. Bertram Mills' winter quarters to house his animals. The place was Ascot. This was our new home for quite a long time.

Outside the barracks was a large, hot, empty field surrounded by barbed wire and towers with machine guns. Not a tree. No shadow. Only weeds and dust.

After waiting for a long time without any food or drink some eighty of us were told which barrack to enter. I got B in the Elephant Room, a large hall with layers and layers of wooden boards, three on top of each other. We were told to fill our mattresses with straw, received each two blankets, a cup of tea and some bread and told to go to sleep.

26 June

I was awake during the whole night, and so was everybody else. The open toilets stank and the old men shuffled along trying to empty their poor old bladders, while some of the younger ones slept and snored. I know that such things – and far worse ones – were common all over the world, but this knowledge didn't help me any more than being told that having lost one leg I was lucky not to have lost both.

Breakfast: tea, bread, burnt porridge. No salt, no sugar. Thank God the weather is fine. I cannot imagine how life will be if it should rain. There may have been some 400 of us. Men of seventy and boys: university professors, lecturers, salesmen, doctors, shopkeepers. Ninety per cent, I would say, Jewish refugees.

But now something remarkable did happen: the Jewish will for survival, which had helped the Jews to survive two thousand years of relentless persecution while all the great empires disappeared: Romans, Greeks, Babylonians, Hittites, went into almost automatic action.

Half an hour after breakfast on the field I saw everywhere small groups of eight, ten or more people listening to a man who talked. The system of self-preservation by learning had begun. Went from group to group. Largest group round chap teaching English. Don't know who he is.[1] Don't know anybody.

Someone is teaching French, someone – I could hardly believe it – probably an actor, recited large parts of Goethe's *Faust*. Someone running round camp wearing pullover with Britain written on it. Stopped him. He spoke only English. Why Britain? I said. 'Ran for Britain in the Olympic Games,' he said.

Started drawing, sitting on a rock. Thank God, Diana had put some Indian ink, charcoal, a pen and a block of writing paper in my suitcase. Had to discover a new technique. I had done little drawing before, being only interested in painting.

Midday: rotten food. Just eatable if very lumpy. Frightful. Typically English. Evening: concert: two fiddlers, very old piano. Started with 'God Save the King' and finished with 'God Save the King'. What must poor Commander think of us? 'Funny Nazis,' he must have said to himself. Somebody told me that our predecessors had been Nazis, mainly prisoners from German ships.

NEW CHAPTER

Here the first part of the journal comes to a sudden end. I must have lost the pages because I kept it regularly. All I can remember between then and the next entry, 7 September (two months and some ten days later), is that we spent about four weeks in the beastly camp, that we did not receive one single letter from home in spite of the fact that London was only twenty-five miles away, a totally unnecessary cruelty, that the letters we were allowed to write home never arrived (the censor probably put them in the wastepaper basket), that after four weeks we were sent to the I.O.M. [Isle of Man] Hutchinson Camp where we arrived surrounded by guards with fixed bayonets. The camp consisted of a block of some thirty to forty small boarding houses which the Army had taken over having forced the wretched landladies to abandon their homes (see *The Making of an Englishman*).

7 September
Rawicz played. Nearly cried when he played 'Smoke Gets in My Eyes'. This I heard in Tossa del Mar when I met Diana. Terribly depressed about Halifax speech. Schwitters recites his Dada poems. What a marvellous story teller this man is. Don't mind how often I have heard the story before. Can always listen like one listens to music.

Wake up during night. Somebody in the next house screams, 'They are coming. They are coming. They want to kill me. Help! Help!' And another voice: 'Don't be afraid. Sleep. Sleep.'

8 September
Am so depressed that I cannot eat.

Talked with Georg Ehrlich and Professor Jacobsthal. Professor William Cohn joined us and talked about the difference between China and Japan (Genius versus Talent). Earliest museum in the world (ca. 750 AD). Nara, Japan.

9 September
Again this terrible, ghastly, sickening depression.

Nothing will help. No courage, nor logic. The black cloud will not disperse. I hate seeing people. Rumours about bad air-raids over London, which can only mean that I will not be released for weeks and weeks.

10 September

Calmer, during the day, but neurotic towards evening. Did three drawings (Death carrying the child on his shoulder, Christ surrounded by skulls).

Evening: Talk by Georg Ehrlich, the sculptor, the best one left since Charoux, thanks to his friendship with the Astors, was released. (Form is everything. The egg, the ear, a shell.)

11 September

Best day for weeks. (Why, I don't know. Depressions like clouds come and go.) Schwitters goes on painting me. Explains my face as a mask. Asks me 'Do you think "ich bin total verkracht?" Do you think I am completely bankrupt as a painter?' 'Of course not,' I said with as much conviction as I could muster. The trouble is that his figurative paintings are so poor that they wouldn't be accepted by the R.A. And so – to hide his bad paintings – he has to go back to Dada Art and Dada is as dead as the dodo. Isn't life Dada enough?[2] Excellent talk by Professor William Cohn: the Japanese collector, Shintoism. Art in Gandara, India, timeless. No history, mainly mythology.

12 September

Good day. One drawing. In the afternoon: talk myself.

13 September

All calm. Schwitters tells his marvellous stories. 'How the bed bugs came into the Royal Academy in Hanover', the black, beautiful 'glass' which he discovered and which he left on the hot oven, the poisoned mushrooms which he ate.

After the talk he gave me a short story which he had written for me entitled: 'The story of the flat and round painter.'

14 September

Best day since my internment. (Exhibition: Ehrlich, Krämer, Fechenbach, Markiewicz, Kahn, Blensdorf, Hamann.)

15 September

Great success of exhibition. Captain Jurgensen turned up. Much ignored. Second lecture by Cohn. Japanese artists sits on the ground when painting, the Chinese in a chair. As almost the same eight traditional landscapes. He never works from nature. The picture is created from memory (like all of mine). Enormous importance of material particularly brushes, paper, ink.

16 September
Terrible weather; and, of course, terribly depressed. Hate seeing the same faces again and again. Cohn's third lecture: Indian civilization. Relations with Mesopotamia. Aryans, Alexander, Scythians, Huns, Moslems, British. Art mainly religious.

17 September
The exhibition closes. Professor Cohn released, which is marvellous for him and dreadful for us. (Professor Heinemann, Misch, Goldmann, Rothfels, Mendelssohn-Bartholdy are still with us, thank God). Two hundred newcomers are expected tomorrow.

Professor Goldmann talks to me about the Etruscan language. He believes he knows now two or three words for certain.

18 September
Bad news from London. Did three drawings. Arnoldi our cook and almost certainly the only Nazi in our camp, found out singing: '*Heut fahren wir gegen Engelland.*' He stands often in the window looking out for the Nazis to land. Showed him my drawings. He was greatly disturbed: 'Why is the child so alone? Where is his father?' And this from a man who, when in power, would have no hesitation to have all of us, including women and children, executed.

19 September
Letter from Diana who misses me badly. Child doing well.
Nothing else to report.

20 September
Got Baudelaire's poems from Diana. Evening: Unger speaks about Greek philosophy.

21 September
Beautiful clear day. Friedenthal speaks about Elizabethan Theatre. Didn't know there were two barrels next to the stage into which men pissed.

22 September
Calm. One drawing. Goodbye to Professor Goldmann, Pfeiffer, Krämer. Hard to hide my jealousy. Why can they go and not I? In the evening Professor Jacobsthal, Wellesz came to see me. Evening: Concert. Chopin, Magic Flute. Farewell Concert for Professor Glas, our only good musician. Oh hell, oh misery.

23 September
One drawing. Talk: 'Shall the artist describe his own age?' Violent discussion.

24 September
Olden dead.[3] Friedenthal talks about Cortez.

25 September
Today it's three months since I was interned. I remember how Diana and I smiled when we said goodbye. Schwitters suggests we should have our own camp flag. Blue, white, red. Blue: blue pencil, white: paper, red: red tape. A new decoration. The O.B.H. Order of British Hospitality. Rawicz and Wellesz play together, setting the following text to music:

> Intern the lot – drum, drum, drum
> Release the lot – drum, drum, drum
> Intern, release – drum, drum, drum
> Intern the lot
> Why not?

26 September
Friedenthal continues with his lecture on Cortez's conquest of Mexico. One drawing. Nothing of interest.

27 September
Wonder why so many people have eczema all over their face? Commander starts 'collecting' art, followed by Sergeant Major! We all have to make contributions which I do willingly. Both are decent chaps.

28 September
Nothing to report.

29 September
Professor Jacobsthal released. Returns to Oxford. In the evening Professor Isaaks talks about 'History of Therapy', but I can hardly listen. How is life in London? What do people think? When will I emerge from barbed wire? Nothing else interests me. Wonder what others feel? There are some 1500–2000 people in our camp of which I know perhaps fifty to sixty. There are quite a few who seem to be quite happy. Businessmen, tradesmen. I see them playing cards, smoking, receiving enormous food parcels from home. We, the elected few, avoid them like they avoid us. They belong to a world of which I know nothing. There are some who speak only Yiddish, some only Polish. There may be, hidden away, even some Nazis. We know that there are spies who inform the Commander (one I know). We know that the Communists have cells, meet regularly and spy on everybody, including themselves.

30 September
Letter from Francis Klingender. (He lives rent free in my London house together with his girl friend Hetta.) Asks me if he can offer shelter to people who have lost their homes in the blitz. Write at once that he is free to do so.[4]

1 October
Grey, menacing sky. Fear of winter. Wrote one poem. Read Lin Yutang whose book keeps up my morale.

2 October
Went to see Schwitters who is painting me. When I approached the house where he moved to get a small attic room to himself, I heard terrific barking, which surprised me because neither women nor dogs were admitted in the camp. I entered, hardly believing my ears. On the ground floor stood a Viennese businessman barking wildly and shaking with rage.

Woo, woo, woo, woo, woo, barked the Viennese as fast as he could.

Woo – woo – woo – answered Schwitters from the top landing, but not half as fast as the Viennese Dachshund, more like an elderly, well mannered Alsatian.

Woo, woo, woo, woo, woo, woo, woo, yelled the Dachshund. Woo – woo – woo – came the dignified reply.

This went on for at least five minutes. Then both dogs retired, each to his room.

When I went up to Schwitters' rather filthy little attic I found a 'kennel' in the middle of the room.

Schwitters obviously had decided that, barking so beautifully, perhaps he was a dog after all. In this belief he had created the 'kennel' which consisted of his table which he had covered with more blankets. Under the table was his mattress and there he slept night after night barking softly before he went to sleep.

The room stank. A musty, sour, indescribable stink which came from three Dada sculptures which he had created from porridge, no plaster of Paris being available. The porridge had developed mildew and the statues were covered with greenish hair and bluish excrements of an unknown type of bacteria. Schwitters, who had the body of a peasant but the head of a Goethe or better of Gerhard Hauptmann, lived and worked there having no studio at his disposal.[5] Then he started to paint me. Having no canvas and no easel he put a large piece of linoleum on a chair (the lino came from the floor of our boarding house – he always carried a sharp knife for this purpose – while the pedestals on which his porridge statues came to rest, came largely from the legs of a piano which he had successfully demolished. (I wonder how much the Government had to pay in compensation to the wretched landladies.)[6] I bought the portrait for what he demanded: five pounds. (This would be at least £100 today.) It was not a masterpiece, but a good likeness and certainly the best of the dozen or more of his paintings on lino.

3 October

My child is three months old today. I invited twenty-six guests and we had a marvellous birthday party with wine and food.

Friedenthal gives last talk on Cortez conquest of Mexico, a story which makes me sick. I don't know who was more horrible, the Aztecs who slaughtered daily hundreds of human beings because the sun needed blood or would die without it and without it the earth; or the Spanish Christians. I think the Aztecs were more terrible considering that thousands of children were slaughtered to satisfy the Rain God: 'And the more the children cried the more rain would fall.'

4 October

Wellesz: Music of Byzantium. He believes that the music came to

Constantinople via Syria and contained a strong element of Jewish Synagogue music, which the Christian Church had taken over from the Jews (like the Church had taken over Passover and Hanukkah).

6 October

Terrible weather.

Ehrlich came and we talked for hours. The artist is the greatest Schnorrer (professional beggar) and parasite. Like pigs they look for pearls in a rubbish heap. Pissarro, Maillol have no hesitation to 'steal' from everywhere. One must let a face speak for itself. Goya did it. He didn't implant his own ideas into the face. He accepted what nature gave him as a gift.

Pastor Crämer told me about the hell he spent in an internment camp called Warth Mill near Manchester and a sadistic Commander who robbed the prisoners of all their belongings.

7 October

Nothing.

8 October

Nothing. Two drawings.

9 October

Weather awful. For days not a single release. No letters from home since one dated September 23rd.

In the evening Zuntz read from the Odyssey.

'Andra moi ennepe, musa polytropon'

It moved me deeply, nearly to tears. When will I see the smoke from my house?

Café full: Blensdorf, Ehrlich, Hamann, Krämer, Franck (with whom I share my room. A fine architect who built High Point in Highgate and many other modern buildings. He belonged to the Tektons.) Wellesz, Pariser, Zuntz, Henning, Sluczewski, Kastner, Friedenthal, Kahn, Hinrichsen, Sohn-Rethel.

10 October

Sun for a few hours. Talk Wellesz: 'Music of the Middle Ages' followed by Friedenthal's 'Contrasts between England and America in the 18th Century'. (Swift, Sterne, Defoe, Locke, Hume, Johnson.) On one side an exuberant, immoral England, facing a narrow, puritanical America.

In the evening Rawicz plays.

Only one drawing.

11 October

Terribly depressed. Homesick. Want to see Diana and my child. Two drawings.

In the evening long discussion about Montaigne (Rousseau, Proust) '*La défaillance du coeur*'. (Proust realizing suddenly, months after his grandmother's death, on seeing her old suitcase that she was really dead.)

Montaigne mentions this too: '*La moindre surcharge brisa la barrière de la patience.*'

Strange man, Pariser. A merchant who knows more about Montaigne than anyone else I have ever met and who, he tells me, is writing a book: 'The Sociology of Fashion'.

12 October

Wellesz, Ehrlich, Pariser, released. I am glad for *them* but what about me? Why can I, who deserved it more than they who never did anything against the Nazis, not be released? Why must I be more and more alone when the best people are going? Can hardly sleep and don't want to eat. Hate the whole place more than ever.

Heard an extraordinary story which happened last Saturday. The air-raid sirens went off shortly after dark. Total black-out everywhere with the exception of the 'Kosher House' where the Orthodox Jews are living. Commander shouted into the megaphone: put that f…..g light out. No reply. It was Sabbath. Nobody could lift receiver. Commander, raging mad, sends messenger along. Messenger wants to switch lights off. Jews ask him: Are you a Jew? Messenger says yes. Jews tell him they can't allow such a sin. Messenger returns to Commander – who bites carpet. Howls with rage. Tries to find non-Jew. Discovers one half-Jew. Sends him along. Sirens. Air warning over.

Evening: Zuntz talks about history of Bible. Text by Esra after return from Babylon; Septuaginta; Codex Vaticanus; Sinaicus; Alexandria.

Sleep without real sleep. What does London look like? Are there taxis? Telephones?

14 October

Two sketches. Bad toothache. Hate seeing dentist. There are a few wholly illiterate men in camp. One of them asks Captain Jurgensen for cigarette. Jurgensen gives him six pennies. 'Hoi,' shouts man, 'Hoi! They cost seven pennies.'

Overheard marvellous conversation piece. Two rather slimy individuals talking to each other. One of them says to other, 'A man like you who has had his fingers in white slave trade, should he be most careful with British Nationalism?'

Evening: Zuntz. Homer.

15 October

Terrible night. No post. Evening cabaret. Schwitters makes us all laugh, even me who doesn't feel like laughing. Perhaps something good will happen tomorrow. It's the 16th (4 x 4, Diana's lucky number and mine is 4.)

Dentist pulled my tooth out which might mean release. Pure superstition, of course.

16 October

Rawicz released. (Oh hell, lucky devil.) Somebody thinks they put bromide in our tea to keep us calm and sexless. Schwitters' ghastly son, who never talks to his father and calls himself Schwitters-Guldahl, because he is ashamed of his father, has applied for release. Reasons: he has been told from 'reliable' sources that lack of intercourse loosens one's teeth and some of his teeth are getting loose.

A bloody little liar.

18 October

Bad news: no release expected for a long time.

Talk with Friedenthal who, quite rightly, points out what extraordinary microcosm this is! A lion tamer. Old 'British' Sea Captains who can't speak a word of English [German] but failed to take out naturalization papers. Müller-Blensdorf who was four years a sailor, returned to England via Gibraltar after end of First War, bubonic plague on board; 2,500 dead thrown overboard.

19 October

Am I going mad? Am suffering from terrible giddiness. Black desire of the soul. Real despair.

Two drawings. Child and gallows. Child and priest.

Friedenthal talks about America-England (a man before a sailor, a sailor before a foreigner, a foreigner before a dog, a dog before a soldier).

20 October

Weather appalling. Worst depression I have ever had. Don't want to see anybody but forced myself to go to Dr Wiener's lecture on Metternich.

21 October

Depression. Too ill to work. Evening air-raid against Liverpool. Fires visible. Hear that the Home Office will release 'eminent' artists. Am I 'eminent' enough? Eminent at all?

22 October

Beautiful October day. Try to fight depression by telling myself that millions suffer more, that I am damned lucky to be alive, that I am a bloody coward, a spoiled man who has – compared with others – a good life – nothing helps. Reason is powerless. If only I had a date: you'll be free in six months, six years, *I could settle*. But the uncertainty is so hard to bear, the injustice of my internment, the releases, this makes one despair. Makes one envious, which is a nasty thing but easy to understand. Talk about China. Mongols, Moghuls in India. 9 April 1241, Liegnitz. In Austria they came as far as Neustadt. Adriatic as far as Ragusa. Returned to Asia 1242.

23 October

Nothing to report. Heard stories that Jack Bilbo is in another camp and gave lecture on 'Why I kept quiet for so long. Jack Bilbo alias Traven'. What a fantastic liar this man is. A fat, enormous eunuch, a man who never will grow up living in a world of fantasy. (Real name: Baruch. Comes from Berlin.)

Wrote a book 'Carrying a gun for Al Capone'. Confessed to police when arrested as self-confessed gangster that it was pure invention. When war started I read in *Evening Standard*: 'One of the most important men for war effort will be Jack Bilbo who fought in Spain, Paraguay and Mexico. He says he will be either machine-gunner or fighter pilot.' He never fought, much too fat. Met him in Spain where he ran a night club (in Sitges). Always carried a whip.

24 October
Unable to think, to work, but recite poems to myself which I remember.

First: Hölderlin: '*Patmos*.' (A wonderful work. If God would write poetry He could not have done better. Seriously: He is one of the world's greatest poets.) Tried to translate into English, but gave up. My English is not good enough. And how can one translate:

> *'Die Mauern stehen – sprachlos und kalt*
> *Im Winde klirren die Fahnen.'*

which is so moving that each time I read it I begin to shiver.

> 'The walls are standing speechless and cold
> In the wind icy flags tinkle.'

How can one translate '*klirren*'? The noise which frozen sheets make when moved by the wind? It's a 'glassy' noise. No word for it in English.

How can I give an idea how beautiful Goethe is? Take one single poem, a short one:

> *Über allen Gipfeln*
> *Ist Ruh,*
> *In allen Wipfeln*
> *Spürest du*
> *Kaum einen Hauch;*
> *Die Vögelein schweigen im Walde*
> *Warte nur, balde*
> *Ruhest du auch.*

How can one 'translate' *Du, Ruh* – what use is the dreadful sound: thou? German poetry, not prose, well spoken is pure music. English sounds harsh. It's not a really beautiful language like Italian, French, German. To my ear anyway. And how to give even an idea about his 'divine' poems – and they are 'divine', so divine that I, an atheist, could almost be persuaded to believe in the existence of a God – poems like '*Prometheus*'; '*Grenzen der Menschheit*'; '*An den Mond*'. Reciting Hölderlin, I remembered my beloved Swabia. How beautiful it was. The mediaeval towns. The fountains. Monasteries and abbeys. The Black Forest. Lake Constance. Rhine, Main, Danube, Neckar. The Vineyards. Tübingen, my wonderful old university with the Hölderlin Tower, where he spent over 30 years, insane, *'Von den Göttern entrückt'* (Removed by the Gods). How strange that most of Germany's *'Dichter und Denker'* came from this small, most civilized country, surrounded and influenced by France, Austria, Switzerland, the birthplace of Schiller. Hölderlin, Mörike, Wieland, Uhland, Hauff, David Friedrich Strauss, Hegel, Schlegel, Schelling, Hesse. (Only Goethe was missing!)

And now, nearly crying, I remember thee 'my Swabia'. You never were Nazi. (Only 25% voted for them in the last free election, when I marched through the streets of Stuttgart together with Schumacher, the hero, and Fritz Bauer.)

25 October

No post. Miserable morning. Remember a saying, possibly by Swift: 'Man is not a reasonable animal. He is only capable of reason.' I am, so it seems to me, no more capable of reason. I know I should not be so easily depressed. Have no right to complain while men and women in London are dying in their thousands. But I want to be with them. There I should be, not behind barbed wire like a bloody Nazi. This is the reason for my depression, the injustice and stupidity of the internment, the fact that prosperous businessmen, technicians, speculators were released long before us because they 'were useful for the war effort' but, in true English fashion, not artists nor political refugees. (By the way the first chap almost immediately released was the Zoo's elephant keeper, who left at once because the elephants refused to eat.)

Speaking about the elephant keeper, I talked to a fascinating man who did spend years and years hunting animals for zoos. He is convinced that there are still unknown animals in the forests of the Congo. Speaking about cobras he said it wasn't necessary to take aim. All one had to do was to point the gun in the direction of the snake and then press the trigger. One would always hit the snake in the head because the snake always followed the point of the rifle. He told me another extraordinary story. He worked for a time at a snake farm near Port Elizabeth. Having only one black mamba, the deadliest of all snakes, it was announced in the town that the farm would pay one pound for every black mamba. A few days later two boys arrived with a mamba wrapped up in newspaper. They got their pound and disappeared. A few days later the boys returned with another! Now, he said, he got suspicious. When it got dark he waited near the low fence which surrounded the farm, low because nobody dared to enter. It got dark. The boys appeared, entered the compound waiting to steal the only black mamba (which they already had stolen and sold twice for the third time!).

He said he had no idea why the boys were not bitten. He told a lot of such stories. (How to make shoes from the rubber tree, how to find turtle eggs, etc.) I am convinced he did not lie.

26 October
Am suddenly much calmer. It comes and goes. Did three sketches. Much impressed with Lin Yutang's book *The Importance of Living* which helped me a lot to see things in perspective. Feel almost 'happy'.

27 October
We were allowed to leave the camp and visit the museum (prehistoric, Celtic), a great experience.

28 October
Feel so much better. One drawing, two poems.

In the evening Homer again.

29 October
Grey, cold. Two more poems. Evening with Blensdorf.

Reading: Duc de Lauzun, The Crusaders.[7]

1 November
Dish washing today. My turn. Washed up for hours: Thirty-eight plates, thirty-eight cups, thirty-eight saucers, knives, gravy plates. Plain hell. And to think that a hundred thousand, perhaps millions of people have to do this as a profession. Ill paid, if at all. It teaches me how lucky I have been. Lucky that I was born in January 1901 and not in December 1900 or I would have been called up and I might have died fighting for what was later Nazi Germany like my uncle, Lt. Karl Elsas, a delightful man who was killed at Bapaume. Lucky that I was so strong or I would have died of peritonitis at the age of twenty-one (even so it was touch and go). Lucky that the hood of my car was down when the car

skidded on black ice, overturned and I flew through the air and landed, without even a scratch, in a snowdrift. Lucky that Dill, the Nazi Deputy Minister of Justice, warned me (why?) and gave me time to escape to France. Lucky that Diana came to Tossa del Mar, that by pure chance my postcard to Thomas Cook (one of six which I did send to Granada, Seville, Toledo etc.) reached her, that my effort to join the International Brigade failed, that Diana married me – where would I be now? Dead ages ago.

No, I have no right to complain but, fool as I am, I do. How many millions have died and are dying? Many far better than I. Future Nobel Prizewinners, scientists, artists. No, all depends on luck. Luck when you are conceived: the right sperm meeting the right egg. The right place. The right environment – everything depends on it.

> 'Every man is lucky if his luck is good
> and hard if it goes badly.
> They most excel if they are loved by the Gods.' (Simonides)

This reminds me of a story told by a distinguished Spanish artist: Francesco Galli Fabra, who had been Director of the Prado and, if I remember rightly, of the Museum of Barcelona. Galli, an old friend of ours, had escaped from Spain. One morning he told me he got a telephone call from one of his friends who said, 'Galli, I wanted to fly to Paris but I have had a terrible dream, I dreamed the plane was crashing in flames. I am frightened. I don't want to go. I am superstitious. Would you like to go to Paris for nothing?' Galli went to Paris, had a wonderful time and returned safely home. His friend went to his office in the main street of Barcelona when a woman jumped out of the fifth floor of a house, fell on him and killed him. She survived.

All of us are furious. Böhm, a nice chap, got three days in prison for giving a flower to his fiancée who stood outside the barbed wire. How stupid these bloody bureaucrats are, particularly our Commander, Major X [Daniel], an insurance agent in private life.

2 November

Concert. (Bach, Mozart, Beethoven.) Glas, Furth, Sluczewski performing.

Saw my friend, the big game hunter again. What an extraordinary, fantastic man! He showed me his chest. In the front an enormous scar: the claws of a lion. In the back a hole, big enough to put my fist in, the horn of a rhino. (He treated all his injuries himself making a paste containing permanganate and other ingredients which I forget. Everything healed without any help by a doctor.)

Wish I could remember more of his stories: how to enter a cage full of lions. The lions must retreat by pure willpower. No whip necessary. According to him the black mamba is green when young. He says he had never any friends but was used to being alone and in constant danger.

He had cut with a razor blade the best window painting in our camp,[8] better than the professional artists: monkeys climbing palm trees, giraffes, lions. Primitive but beautifully observed.

3 November

Went to see Dr Streliska, an excellent graphologist with whom I had discussed graphology before. Told me that he has a collection of some thousand prints of human palms, some of them from people who had died a violent death.

Showed him a letter from Diana, whom he has never met. Amazingly correct. Revealing certain trends in her character only known to me.

4 November

Four years ago Diana and I got married and by doing so she saved my life and made it possible for me to be a painter. Without her I would almost certainly have died either fighting in Spain or in a concentration camp. What courage she had to break with her whole family and to commit what Sir Henry called 'social suicide'.

Marvellous day. Was allowed to leave the camp with Dr. Bersu, an archaeologist, looking for burrows and manganese. Told him that I had begun to collect Roman 'treasures' at the age of ten and that I had bought a fibula and an arrow head from a little boy called Balz. 'My God,' said Bersu, 'now I know why so much did disappear when I and his father dug out a Roman kiln.'

5 November

Dr. Streliska looked at my hand and my writing. Have met him twice before and he had never seen my paintings.

This is what he said. (I would say 90% correct.) Abnormally strong sensitivity. Tendency to melancholia, pessimistic outlook, possibly inherited from my mother. Strong sense of justice. Tendency to pedantry but mainly to create order, fearing chaos.

As a painter, love for architectural subjects: walls, towers, streets. Dislike of strong colours like red. Highly poetical, romantic. Colours subdued.

Strong feminine trend. Easily hurt, easily offended. Insecure: careful with money. Good, but strongly suppressed business instinct, powerful childhood impressions which provided a stimulus and a desire to escape. Sadistic tendencies sublimated in art. Erotically inhibited: cautious in approach to strangers. It takes time before you trust them.

Biological longevity but less strong vitality.[9] Streliska said that he had never seen the hand and writing of any artist without discovering something abnormal, i.e. sadism, masochism, fetishism. (Many surgeons sublimate their desire for inflicting pain by using it to relieve pain just like the artist triumphs over his abnormality by increased sensitivity in his art.)

7 November

Carl Ludwig Franck who shared my room since we arrived has been released. Alas, it made me even more unhappy, partly because I lose a good companion – we never had any quarrel under difficult conditions and endless tensions – but also because I was envious. We all are, because we all suffer from the terrible daily torture known as 'release'. Why is he going home? How long will I be here? Of course one does one's best to hide one's feelings, but we all know how one feels and Franck knows only too well how I feel. We gave him the usual farewell party and then he left, the lucky bastard.

8 November

Zuntz released. All the best people go. Farewell party. (What will happen when I will be more or less alone?) Of course there are still hundreds left, but will I find so many congenial friends again, so many distinguished men? Of course, there must be many interesting people worth knowing in this multitude, this microcosm which contains famous men and illiterates (we have at least half a dozen in the camp), honest men and real crooks and gangsters, but it takes time to find out who they are. One thing is amazing: during the whole period I have been here I have not seen one single fight[10] which is unusual considering the density of the population with some thirty to forty per house and often five or six sharing a room. Perhaps the fact that there was no drunkenness made a lot of difference and also that the majority of prisoners were Jews, many of them educated men and not prone to aggression. In the evening Friedenthal talked about Elizabethan theatre, a brilliant performance considering that he had not a single book at his disposal.

9 November

Twenty-two years since the revolution in Germany, since I saw the red flag flying in Stuttgart, the red sailors arriving from Kiel who tried to establish a Soviet state in Württemberg. The abdication of our good old king. Who would have told me then that twenty-two years later I would find myself on the Isle of Man? Finished two more drawings and translated as well as possible with my little English some lines from Schnitzler's play *Paracelsus*:

Es fließen ineinander Traum und Wachen,
Wahrheit und Lüge. Sicherheit ist nirgends.
Wir wissen nichts von andern, nichts von uns;
Wir spielen immer, wer es weiß, ist klug.

Dream and waking
Truth and falsehood merge into each other
Nowhere is certainty
We know nothing of others
Nor of ourselves
We are playacting always
Wise is he who knows it.

10 November

Have a new room-mate, a chap called Runkel, a blond Aryan who could be a Nazi but is a fanatical Commie instead. (I hate both. I know too much of them.) Never trust a Commie. To save 'Mother Russia' (*ex Oriente lux*) they would commit every crime: treason, murder. God, how long I argued with the bloody fools not to vote for Hitler. 'No,' they said, 'we got our instructions' (from Moscow, of course). 'We must bring him into power. He is only dangerous in opposition. Once in power he will be finished in six months and then it's our turn.' The blond beast asked me if I would mind if he would sleep in my room. I said 'yes' (what else could I do?). He informed me that before asking me the Party had made enquiries about me and they were satisfactory! (Hurrah!)

Then he started cleaning the room which Franck had left in a terrible state. A cushion had exploded and there were feathers everywhere which Franck, normally elegant and clean but now rather dirty, had not bothered to sweep up. Well, Runkel washed and cleaned everything, lined his books up like soldiers and began to prepare himself for the time when he would return to red Germany as a Commissar. We didn't talk much because, as he was only interested in politics, I had nothing to say to him. One must never talk to a Commie about Stalin nor to an Arab about Allah. It's a waste of time.

11 November

Went to Hamann, the sculptor who had got hold of some clay and gave lessons. Started a small figure but didn't like sculpting very much. I am just a painter and nothing else.

Went to see Schwitters. No dogs this time. The room stank even more than usual. Poor Schwitters had fallen over his enormous chamber pot, 'full to the brim' as he said, and spilled the whole lot over the floor. Terrified the liquid would go through the ceiling, he used everything 'handy' to stop the flow and clean up the mess. The porridge sculptures had even longer beards and looked like overripe Stilton.

12 November

Storms, rain, fog. Read *Robinson Crusoe* and *Gulliver's Travels*. Quite a revelation. Didn't know it was such a powerful political satire having only read it as a children's book ages ago. Krämer told me that a man in his house had been interned because the police had found a diary in which he had written 'Exchange British Queen against Italian Queen'. The man was a beekeeper and Italian Queen bees are better.

13 November

Went to Hamann working on my sculpture (a female nude, of course!). Don't like it.

Returning home I found Runkel studying. He knows that he has little chance to be released but he seems to be perfectly contented waiting for the day of his triumphant return to Soviet Germany and

Armageddon. He is slowly getting on my nerves – like a married couple irritated by small, repetitive things – particularly how he brushes his teeth: left – right, left – right, up – down, up – down.

It's like a military operation. And how he gargles and spits the water out: pscht – pscht – pscht.

14 November

We open our new café, a room with laundry hanging across the room. Unger released. Farewell party. If only I wouldn't be so envious. Why Unger? Why not me?

15 November

Arnoldi, our Nazi cook, is beginning to be more and more unpleasant. It must be dreadful for him to live here surrounded by Jews, waiting, waiting not for release but for the Nazi fleet to arrive. He made a dreadful scene because I had eaten a piece of cake without first asking his permission.

16 November

Friedenthal's Shakespeare. Group of English actors in Germany, particularly in Brunswick. Strange figure of the Duke Heinrich Julius who, influenced by these English groups, wrote a dozen 'Shakespearian plays' in prose (1590–1620). Marlowe, Kyd, whose *Spanish Tragedie* was a marvellous success.

Ben Jonson, Shakespeare in England; Cervantes, Lope de Vega in Spain, Montaigne in France. Nothing in Germany, which had no world literature until Goethe.

17 November

Two lino cuts. Solomonski sings. Furth plays flute.

Try to translate a lovely German poem (author unknown; date: 14/15th Century?).

Es fiel ein Reif in der Frühlingsnacht
Er fiel auf die zarten Blaublümelein
Sie sind verwelket, verdorret.

Ein Jüngling hatte ein Mädchen lieb
Sie flohen heimlich von Hause fort
Es wußt' weder Vater noch Mutter

Sie sind gewandert hin und her
Sie haben gehabt weder Glück noch Stern
Sie sind verdorben, gestorben.

A frost fell in a night of spring
It fell on the blue flowerlets
They faded away and withered

A lad once loved a maiden fair
Both ran away from house and home
Neither father knew it nor mother

They wandered hopelessly here and there
No lucky star shone anywhere
They died, they perished in despair.[11]

18 November

A major in uniform appeared making a recruiting speech for the Pioneer Corps. Quite a few younger men, knowing that they had no chance of being released, joined. They all are getting British papers, they have to anglicize their names so that if they fall into German hands they couldn't be shot as traitors. Levi will be Lloyd, Goldmann Gould and Rosenthal Rossdale, I presume. It would be funny if it wasn't so serious.

Gave a talk on the history of the Huguenots in England. Well received.

19 November

Exhibition opened by Commander. (Hamann, Blensdorf, Uhlman, Weissenborn, Schwitters, Krämer, Solomonski, Kahn, Markiewicz, Fleischmann, Fechenbach showing.) Evening Concert. Lieder by Schubert, Brahms; Sonata by Bach (forget which).

20 November

Schwitters talks. Tremendous success. He repeats his old stories, but nobody minds to hear them again. How the bedbugs came into the Royal Academy in Hanover, how he escaped from Norway with his six white mice, how he wanted to prove that he was more clever than nature by eating poisonous mushrooms, the copper nail, Lanke Trrgl, Ooka, Ooka and so on. Am certain that he doesn't mind being interned: no money worries for him, no blitz, free food, a studio. What could be better. There must be hundreds of people like him, people of whose existence I have no idea, who would hate to be free with all the difficulties and dangers that freedom implies for them: money problems, earning a living, finding shelter.[12]

For such people it's a holiday in fresh air. Like the TB patients in Mann's *Magic Mountain*, they don't want to return to reality. They are living in a world of which I know little or nothing, just like we in Hampstead have not the slightest idea what is happening in Kentish Town or Stepney or across the river. Of course I see them talking to each other, playing cards, mainly poker, but they avoid us as we avoid them – by instinct. They know and we know that we are living next to each other but worlds apart. It could be Hong Kong or Harlem or Timbuktu. I have no idea how they spend their days apart from talking and eating. Are they reading? Have they any interests? I don't know, worst of all, I don't care. They have faces but I wouldn't remember one of them.

21 November

Runkel is getting more and more on my nerves. Not that I can complain. He is always polite, politeness personified, and politeness so icy, so devoid of any interest, so inhuman that it comes very near to contempt. He gives me the creeps. For him, I don't exist. I am just another political enemy who has not seen the true light. A heretic or capitalist, with whom – *faute de mieux* – he has to share a room and who has to be tolerated. God forbid that I ever should fall in his hands. He would execute me in the name of liberté. '*Pas de liberté pour les ennemis de la liberté.*' Good old Danton said it, I believe, who lost his head, which reminds me that I must read Büchner's *Danton* again. What a loss that he died so young, he was only twenty-three if I am not mistaken. He would have been Germany's greatest dramatist. But what do I really know about Runkel? What does one know? What can one know? (What did Paracelsus say: We know nothing about each other, nothing about ourselves. Wise is he who knows it.) Perhaps, if I would make an effort, I might pierce his armour and find underneath a human body made of flesh and blood and not of ice.

Remembered suddenly a story I had completely forgotten told to me by Edith Hoffmann.[13] Her father, Camille Hoffmann, was Press Attaché at the Czech Embassy, when shortly after the Reichstag Fire a leading Communist (whose name I have forgotten) arrived at the Embassy with a large suitcase imploring him to hide it, which Camille did. Years passed and nobody came to claim it. Then Munich came. The Embassy started to burn all the papers when Hoffmann suddenly remembered the suitcase full, or so he believed, of secret Party papers. He got the suitcase, forced the lock and out came ... whips, high-heeled women's boots, bras, false bosoms etc., etc.

I wonder what I would find forcing the lock of Runkel's suitcase? In the evening Captain Jurgensen asked me to see him. He wanted to know what I knew about Jack Bilbo. Was he a gangster, a hero of the Spanish Civil War, did he command a tank regiment? I told him what I knew, Jurgensen laughed and laughed. It was great fun.

23 November

Saw Hamann. His head bandaged. Asking him what had happened to him he said he had been dreaming that a barber had cut him so badly that he was covered with blood. He woke up, dressed himself and had just finished when a large lump of the ceiling crashed on his head cutting him badly.

24 November

One linocut. Read for the fifth time Stendhal's *Rouge et Noir*, (I prefer it to the *Charterhouse of Parma*). What a wonderful, brilliant writer he is. How subtle, how modern. Have now quite a small library: *Le grand Meaulnes*, Carcopino's *Daily Life in Ancient Rome*, a magnificent description of Imperial Rome with its dirt, filth, noise, narrow, dangerous streets, its fabulous wealth and horrible poverty, its slaughterhouse (the Coliseum). I never liked the Romans. What killers they were. (Who wasn't and who isn't? Look what's going on now!) Men will never cease killing and torturing each other. Never. Never. *South Wind* by Norman Douglas. A minor masterwork but still a masterwork. (Met Douglas before the war at Venice. He told me he went to school with my father, which I can't believe.)

Wuthering Heights (difficult to read, my English is not very good), but the book is most impressive. Almost frightening: terrifying. *Pride and Prejudice* I am afraid is still lost on me. I tried before, I cannot understand why so many of my English friends adore Jane Austen. It's such a small, snobbish, class-ridden, rather dull world. So narrow, so arrogant towards the lower classes (they don't even exist). The girls all out for rich husbands. No real passion, only '*amour raisonnée*'. Perhaps one has to live a long time in England, a safe, prosperous island, before understanding Jane Austen.

A dead day. Runkel now brushes his teeth three times a day. Morning, after lunch, evening.

25 November

Today is the fifth month since I was interned. (Why?)

Bad news from London.

26 November

Nothing. Nothing. Nothing.

27 November

The whole camp went to the cinema. Quite a sensation. Not a single guard came with us. That nice Sergeant Major told the Commander that he would personally guarantee there would be not a single incident and that guards were unnecessary. And he was right.

28 November

Nothing. Am too depressed to keep up the diary.

29 & 30 November

Everybody has only one interest: will he be home for Christmas? Nobody mentions it. But I can see it written on almost every face. Evening: Friedenthal talks about Handel.

1 December

December! Have not done any work for days. Suffer from giddiness.

6 December

Henning released. Attend a few lectures.

(Dr Bersu: the history of the Isle of Man; Friedenthal: Haydn.)

10, 11 & 12 December

Nothing. All I do is wait. Waiting until the clock strikes 5.00 when the names of the released are announced, returning to my room sick with despair. Nothing seems to help. It's no good telling myself again and again that millions and millions are dying and starving, that my life, *sub specie aeternitatis*, is without the slightest significance, that I, like everyone else before me and after me, will disappear without leaving a trace, that our universe will disappear, that we all are megalomaniacs who prefer to believe that they are probably insignificant [significant]. (We have to or how could we bear life? We have to pretend that our life is important and makes some sense, which it doesn't.) Nothing helps. No reason, no logic. I am powerless against the turning of the screw, the daily torture known as release. I may be here for months, for years. Like a bear who starts to dance when he hears music because it reminds him of the pain he suffered when they burnt the soles of his feet, I start dancing when I hear the sound of voices announcing the names of the released and collapse when the music stops. I don't think I am a despicable coward. True, I am not used to real pain but I am certain I could bear it easier if all of us were in the same boat, if there were no exceptions, no privileged classes nor such terrible injustices. I would accept my fate because I had to accept it like everybody else. One other difficulty is that one cannot show one's true feelings to others but has to assume an air of gaiety, cynicism, stoicism, hiding one's sufferings so that others should not suffer more than they do. Was it Pindar who said: 'Man's life is a day. What is he? A shadow in a dream is man.'

13 December
Nothing.

14 & 15 December
Nothing.

16 December
Nothing.

17 December
Friedenthal talks about the history of photography. (Bacon, Leonardo, Camera Obscura, Diorama etc.) It's extraordinary what grows inside this man's head. As far as I know he knows it all by memory, having no specialized books at his disposal.

18 December
Fifteen men released. Fifteen!!!

Have given up working, a foolish thing to do because work is the only help against *'Die schwarze Sucht der Seele'*. Nor does it matter very much. I have done some 200 drawings, many of them really good, and important as historical documents of our time. And I wrote a dozen poems.

I am just demoralized. Darling Diana would say: pull yourself together and go for a brisk walk. Got a letter from her in which she told me that a German aeroplane had dropped eleven bombs round our cottage in plain daylight, including one one-thousand pounder. Only some plaster came off. Only! Which reminded me of a letter by Mme de Staël to Constant. 'Dear Benjamin, do come to dinner tonight. It's a small party. Only Goethe and Schiller are coming!!'

19–23 December
No more hope of release before Christmas.

24–25 December
We, some twenty survivors, celebrated Christmas. Everyone made a tremendous effort and even I who loathes Christmas because it brings back true the Germany I loved so deeply, sincerely; the old mediaeval towns, the old market places with the hundreds of little candlelit stalls, the peasants selling rosehip jam and sausages made from quince, the noise of the horse-drawn sledges, the thousands and thousands of Christmas trees, the beauty of the glittering snow and stars, the trumpeters blowing their trumpets from the top of the church towers, my mother at the piano playing and singing 'Stille Nacht' – God how wonderful it was, the only really beautiful memory in my childhood – even I did not feel too unhappy. We got an excellent dinner and we sang Christmas carols, Jews and non-Jews alike. Even I, a non-believer, an atheist since the age of 16 when already then I came to the conclusion that there could not be an all-loving, all-powerful God, a God who accepted the murder of his son without lifting a finger – even I was deeply moved.

26 December
Weissenborn, who had done so much work for all of us, released. Attended the farewell party.

27, 28 & 29 December
Nothing.
30 December

Jurgensen wanted to see me. He asked me a few questions which I cannot remember. Suddenly he said, 'Do you want to go home?' I couldn't speak. 'Do you want to go home?' he repeated with a smile. This time I understood. I didn't say anything. Didn't want to cry.

Met Krämer. Had to tell him that I was released. He congratulated me, poor devil. I know only too well what he felt. Couldn't bear to give a farewell party.

Runkel clicked his heels, '*Auf Wiedersehn in Deutschland*', he said.

31 December

Left for home. Travelling by train to London. Felt very strange in a foreign world. Couldn't believe that I was free, that I could move about freely. I had the strange illusion that everybody stared at me, that everybody knew I was an 'enemy alien' and had been a prisoner, but nobody bothered about me.

The clock struck midnight when I stood outside my house in Hampstead. It was still 1940 when I arrived; one minute later a New Year had begun. I knocked at the door. There was a light in my bedroom; it took some time before somebody, very cautiously, opened the door. Then Francis came and Hetta in her nighty which was full of holes and Johnny Heartfield and Tutti and a girl called Helga. At first they didn't recognize me because I had grown a blond beard, but then there was a tumultuous welcome.

Next day I left for Essex, met Diana and saw my child for the first time. I just cried. It was Caroline, who appeared in *Captivity*,[14] who was eternally victorious, triumphant – and beautiful.

— — —ooo000ooo— — —

POST SCRIPTUM

Here ends this diary which I read recently for the first time: thirty-eight years and one month after my release. It brought back hundreds of things I had completely forgotten: the names of the men I had met, most of them now dead, the incidents, the joys and the misery. Many things I have completely forgotten and which are not mentioned in this diary, i.e. did we get newspapers? Were there radio sets? Had I more than one suit? How much did we know about the war? Was alcohol permitted? When was Friedenthal released?

All this is forgotten. What I have never forgotten was the shock of my arrest, the cruelty not to have been allowed to be with my wife who expected daily her child, the humiliation to be driven through the streets of Douglas, Isle of Man, surrounded by guards and stared at by the population as if I was a captured Nazi, the first weeks in Ascot without receiving a single letter, the muddle, the stupidity, the overcrowding and, most of all, the torture known as release, which began in Douglas. On the other side: what luck I then had to have been a member of one of the finest universities I have ever attended, the wonderful lectures, discussions, the genuine friendship between men who all knew that they depended on each other, the lack of friction and egotism in spite of unavoidable tensions, the courage, the sense of humour and even sometimes the fun and the realization that this was a unique experience and that one could be proud to belong to an elite of the human race. The most vivid picture which even today I can still see closing my eyes is the picture of hundreds of men carrying chairs going to lectures. Nothing seemed to me so magnificent and encouraging. Afterwards some of us met from time to time in a London café but this stopped soon. The only people I met fairly regularly were Krämer, who is now dead, Hamann who died too and Friedenthal who is over 80 but, I believe, still alive.[15] Friedenthal's book on Goethe has been an outstanding success. Once I went to Oxford where I met Wellesz, Cohn and Jacobsthal. All were very friendly but very professional, very distinguished. We were no more in the same boat.

— — —ooo000ooo— — —

THE DRAWINGS

All the 200 drawings were done during the six months of my internment. A few were done in Ascot but most on the Isle of Man, often in difficult circumstances, i.e. a suitcase serving as a table, no table being in existence in my room, shortage of paper; I had to use toilet-paper and newspaper until I got a block of writing paper. As material, Indian ink, pen, charcoal.

The drawings fall in three groups:

A) Topographical: the camp near Ascot which was Bertram Mills' winter quarters, seen from outside and inside, a group of Jewish prisoners; Dr. Zuntz reading from Homer, with me and Rawicz listening, and a Jew reading the Talmud by candlelight.

B) Pure fantasy dedicated *'à mon enfant nouveau né'*. It shows the child, holding a balloon, symbol of joy and liberty, marching with sure, unfaltering steps through the valley of death and horror – totally undisturbed, untouchable and triumphant. Death has no dominion over it, on the contrary it plays and dances with him knowing that it is the future.

C) The last group is a bitter and savage attack, not against religion, but against the Church, particularly in Spain which betrayed Christ. Again the child is victorious. It touches the giant of religious abuse, intolerance and cruelty with one little finger and the monster topples over as if made of cardboard.

Captivity appeared in 1946. In spite of excellent notices it was a commercial flop. Everybody wanted to forget the war. One last word: I do not know if Captain Jurgensen is still alive. I doubt it. If he is I want to thank him for allowing me, against the rules, to take my drawings with me. On one drawing showing old men, mainly Jewish prisoners, I had written 'After the great British victory in the battle of Golders Green'. All he said was, 'Rather bad taste, Mr Uhlman' – but he allowed me to take it with me.

London, February 1979.

NOTES

As annotated by Fred Uhlman himself in 1979. Ms in possession of Imperial War Museum [DDF, IWM, 78/19/1]; original in Uhlman estate.

1. Later I found out it was Heinz Beran who worked for the Austrian Section of the BBC.
2. Of course, I have been wrong. But I was not alone. Nobody in the camp – and there were quite a few artists and plenty of intellectuals – took him seriously.
3. Who was Olden?
4. I found Francis and Hetta in my bed. They were not alone. There was Johnny Heartfield and Tutti, his girlfriend, and at least two 'blitzed' girls (one had probably lost a door handle, the other her toothbrush). They all paid no rent, no gas, no electricity and my beautiful house was in a mess. I told Francis that if my house was destroyed by a bomb I had to accept this, but I could see no reason why my 'friends' should do this to me and suggested he should find a room which, by the way, was easy, Hampstead being nearly empty. I received a stinking letter in which Francis told me that his efforts to educate me had failed and were doomed to failure, my 'mentality as a property owner' being too stong. Hetta was furious too. She had planted a dozen tulip bulbs round my apple tree and she tried to dig them out, and not to leave them with me. As it was winter she couldn't find them. Since then thirty-eight years have passed and the tulips still appear every year, reminding me of Francis and Hetta. Johnny Heartfield and Tutti stayed on for nearly five more years. (Johnny arrived shortly after Prague was occupied.) They too were our guests, a fact which was carefully suppressed because, being a great hero in East Germany, the fact that a bourgeois family looked after him for years, would have harmed his reputation as a Communist leader.

Many years later they returned to London for a five week visit. They stayed a few minutes' walk away but came not once to see us, and they never wrote a single line.

All of them were fanatical Communists – ready to sign any decree ordering the execution of a million capitalists or two or three (including us) for the good of the party and the creation of an earthly paradise. They were 'paper killers', meaning men who would never have been able to touch a child or a woman but would have signed any decree ordering mass murder. One of my friends Heinrich F. announced in a speech that the whole SA and SS had to be shot after the war and I have no doubt that he meant it. There were 700,000 SS and three to four million SA, he said, 'And all have to be shot. All,' said Heini with a happy smile.

5. Later he got a studio where he started – completely by accident – a fire causing some £2,000 of damage in present-day money.
6. The portrait is now in the Schwitters room of the University Museum of Fine Arts in Newcastle upon Tyne. I wish I had bought a few collages for ten shillings a piece. They fetch now £20,000 each!
7. Have no idea what books they were.
8. The Commander, to save the cost of blackout material, had ordered that all the windows had to be covered with paint.
9. I am writing this in my 79th year and can only say that almost everything Streliska told me about myself and my wife has been correct. He was a memorable man, but I do not know what has happened to him. He never belonged to our circle.
10. There might have been fights indoors. There was none in 'my' house.
11. This is a new translation, the one in the camp being too poor.
12. A well-known German Expressionist Ludwig Meidner implored me to do everything in my power to stop [him] being released. He was so happy and had a wonderful time, he said.
13. Edith Hoffmann, art historian, wrote a biography of Kokoschka whom I knew well. Too well.
14. London: Jonathan Cape, 1946.
15. Schwitters I met frequently. Occasionally he arrived with a beautiful young girl who looked after him. Alas, I never bought his collages for 10 shillings each.

6. *Letters to and from Internment*

1) Telegram to the Commandant of Hutchinson Camp, 20 July 1940

Please inform Fred Uhlman his wife and baby making excellent progress and send him their love – Uhlman

2) Diana Uhlman to Fred Uhlman, undated fragment [c. July 1940]

… to Canada – also Hans and Heinz.[1] I agree it is all senseless – perhaps this fact will gradually penetrate to the minds of other people. I don't think one can expect much more from Papa, his attitude is war is war – and the innocent must suffer with the guilty. I must get back to London and see other people and find some way out – there must be a way.

In the meantime let me know if you have any suggestions of how to be useful – I think usefulness is the only criterion – and in any case nobody could want to be more useful in the fight against Hitler more than you.

Otherwise I have no news for you – life here is very quiet and I feel I'm wasting valuable time.

It's horrible without you and I hate it. Have never felt so lonely – especially when among people who don't understand why one suffers – there is a difference between necessary separation and senseless separation – that isn't helping anyone – & that makes [it] a thousand times more bitter.

All my love darling
Diana

3) Diana Uhlman to Fred Uhlman, 29 October 1940

Bambers Green, Takely, Bishops Stortford.
my darling little Freddy.
I'm so sorry not to have written for a few days but have been very busy with Posy staying here. The A[rtists'] R[efugee] C[ommittee] wrote me that the R[oyal] A[cademy] had recommended all artists about whom the A.R.C. sent favourable reports – so presumably you are among these as they wrote a specially favourable report about you. But I have no definite confirmation that you really have been recommended – though think there can be no doubt. Now we just have to wait and see when the Home Office makes up its mind.

Otherwise there's no news. Michael's flat is really uninhabitable now and some of his things ruined. Michael writes he has heard (but doesn't know if it's true) that people released from internment *can* go to protected areas. I will try and find out if there is any hope.

Posy sends you her very best love. She thinks Caroline is wonderful and my mother says (a) she's an 'aryan' (b) her eyes are like headlamps (c) she has never seen such a remarkable child etc. etc. Posy seems very well.

Thank you for your sweet letters – one in which you talk about my eyes just as if we weren't married – sweet you are.

Forgive a horrible short letter – it's only to tell you we're all well and to bring you all my love and hopes that you can come out soon.

Ever and ever your
Diana

4) Fred Uhlman to Diana Uhlman, from Hutchinson Camp, 31 October 1940

[translated from the original German]
Darling Diana,
I have just received your telegram in which you tell me that the R[oyal] A[cademy] has put me forward for release. I do hope it's true. I have become so anxious that I shall only believe in freedom when I am finally able to cross the street on my own and without a guard, and when I hear a woman's voice again. But even so I can already breathe a sigh of relief. I can at least hope for my release – perhaps as early as November. Let's see to what extent this gives me courage, strength and confidence. I intend to write to Witt today and

ask him whether the Tribunal business is now superfluous. I should much prefer to be released as an 'eminent artist' than as a 'prominent anti-Nazi'. The former will always work to my advantage, the latter – who knows – could prove very harmful at some time in the future. Perhaps Witt will succeed in achieving something. Yesterday I received your letter of 23 October. I do hope that we'll manage to stay in Bambers after my release (that is if I don't have to join something like the A.R.P. [Air Raid Precautions] for if the war goes on much longer I shall have to play an active part in one form or another. I should feel very ashamed if I just sat around.) But let's worry about that later. In the meantime I'll ask the Commander about the protected area issue. I'm very annoyed about Francis, in particular that he hasn't handed over the reviews. As for the old man, you will have to be firm (although he's certainly better than Eastender [*sic*]). I think you will have to have a proper fence built or we'll never be able to plant anything and we may well need Bambers again in the future. I hope it won't get too cold. And how about the transport situation? What will happen if the roads can't be used? I'm not in any position to judge. Cambridge and Oxford are overcrowded. I'm sure you won't find a bed there. I'm so pleased that the baby's doing so well. But does she really look so like me? I just can't calm down. Oh darling, darling! What can we do? I have read a wonderful book, *The Importance of Living* by Lin Yutang (Heinemann). Do read it. It gave me so much pleasure. You will find a great deal of wisdom and truth in it, a great deal of what we have both felt and thought. I would so love to talk to you about it. Well good night.

And love for ever,
Your Fred

5) Diana Uhlman to Fred Uhlman, 5 November 1940

Bambers Green, Takely.
my dearest little Freddy,
I had been hoping for a letter but have not had one since last I wrote.

Yesterday was Nov 4th[2] and I was thinking of you all day and remembering all the anniversaries we have celebrated together with a good meal and a nice bottle of wine. Poor Freddy! Perhaps you thought of me too and the 4 years that are past.

I don't know why it is but I am getting so 'sentimental' about you

– and wanting you back more than ever. Now that there is so much more hope of seeing you soon I am thinking about you the whole time – whereas before I hardly dared to think about you so much because I just used to weep like Caroline. Do you understand? I have no news for you. Life goes on the same as ever. Yesterday rain, this morning sun and lovely autumn mist again. I went for my weekly shopping expedition to Stortford.

My cooking is improving – as well it should, after all this time – and I will make you lovely puddings when you come out!

Must post this now, darling – sorry it's so short, but it brings all my love to you

ever your Diana

6) Fred Uhlman to Diana Uhlman, from Hutchinson Camp, 7 November 1940

[translated from the original German]
Darling Diana,
Franck has just been released. Tomorrow morning he's going home to his wife and child and you can imagine how sad I feel. When am I going to see you again? You and the baby whom you have described so charmingly to me, with eyes 'as big as headlamps' and very 'Aryan' – despite my nose? Perhaps I shall be lucky again as I so often was with you in the past. – Tell me darling, are you very depressed at the moment or very tired? I have noticed that for some time now your handwriting has been 'falling' or 'sinking' and that's a sure sign of depression or great tiredness. Darling Diana, don't make me worry about you. Don't tire yourself out and don't be sad. We are sure to see one another again, we will be very happy – as far as one can be happy – we will laugh a lot for all the things that we once took so seriously such as sherry parties and exhibitions will strike us as comical and we will know that there is nothing nicer and better than being together, understanding one another, walking across a field in the sunshine, reading a good book and watching the clouds. By the way, I spoke to the Intelligence Officer today about the protected area issue but he didn't know anything. I think you will have to ask the Chief Constable what we should do. Michael has written me a very nice letter, please thank him for it – I can't write to him because all my letters are reserved for you. Dick Carline has sent me the *Burlington Magazine* with his article on

negro art (with three photographs from my collection).[3] The day before yesterday I went out 'mining'. We went looking for manganese out in the country. We didn't find much but I spent the day far away in the mountains, in delightful surroundings, guarded by only two soldiers. I had the feeling, at least, of being free for a few hours. Well, darling, I'll close as I always do, in all my sleeping and waking moments: I love you with all my heart. I adore you. God bless you and little Caroline and may we be together soon.

And so much more, so much more, and – and – and yours ever and ever

Fred.

7) Fred Uhlman to Diana Uhlman, from Hutchinson Camp, 12 November 1940

[translated from the original German]
Darling Diana,
I am so grateful to you for your last letter. Not because it answered my 'need for affection' (that too, as usual, and I am not in the least ashamed to admit it) but rather because it was very important for us *both*. You see, in the past we spent every day and virtually every hour together! We would sometimes quarrel as people do quarrel when they have been married a long time and when they are always together (and when they have no serious problems). This is now the first occasion that we have been apart for any length of time and it's the first occasion that we each have time to examine the past and to come to terms with ourselves. I have spent hours and days doing that, and the more I have thought about it, the clearer, the stronger, yes, the more glorious has been the realization of how much I love you, how happy you have made me and how much I have to thank you for. And when I write you 'love letters', they are actually not love letters at all but rather the simple, natural and most urgent expression of my feelings for you, feelings that make me crave to see you again so that I can tell you that I love you, that I – I see this now – have not been understanding enough or kind enough towards you and that I should like to make up for it. (Of course, this partly accounts for why internment is such a torment to me. You see, every time I think of you I am gripped by this desperate wish to talk to you and then I can't wait for the moment when I am with you.) Just as this long absence has been important

for me, so it must have been equally important for you too, and that's why I so need to know how you feel about it all. For if you had not felt my absence to any great degree, if you had not missed me, that would have been very bad, that would have meant that our marriage was empty and impoverished. But as it is, everything is alright. We will often quarrel in days to come (because we are only human), but we have learned much from the present situation and have grown wiser and humbler and very much richer. I am now working again (and am for that reason very much calmer). I have started on a small sculpture and have written six poems that I have illustrated for you with linocuts. Perhaps I'll be able to show them to you in November. Perhaps.

Ever, ever yours
Fred

8) Diana Uhlman to Fred Uhlman, undated fragment [November 1940]

[…] every day that we will hear some definite good news about release. It seems interminable – but I do feel that we may not have very much longer to wait.

Poor Winkle. You told me not to send any more parcels about 6 weeks ago – have you been starving – or are things better now?

So tell me - have you really got a little beard – like a *real* artist? Please don't cut it off!

Freddy - I'm tired of waiting *do* come soon. I'm missing you so terribly – nearly 5 months, nearly ½ a year and life is so short!

All love forever
your Diana

* * * *

9) Draft of letter from Fred Uhlman to Lord Croft, undated [early August 1940]

Dear Lord Croft,
I feel I owe you an explanation about the line I sent yesterday.

As you know I have made it a special point to ask for your help only in the most urgent cases during the period of 4 years that I have had the honour to be your son-in-law. As far as I can recollect this was only the case once, when I asked you to assure the Tribunal, who tried me, of the fact that I was definitely Antinazi [*sic*].

When I ventured to address myself to you again yesterday, you may rest assured, that my reasons for doing so were indeed of a serious nature.

As you probably have learnt, I was interned 7 days before my child was born. For 2 weeks I did not know whether my wife was alive, and whether I had a child or not. Today, after 37 days of internment, which in itself seems a grave injustice to me, I have still not received any mail. I do not know how my wife is, what my child looks like, what her name is and whether Diana, who has been left alone in her hard plight, has any news about the well being of her husband.

Perhaps, dear Lord Croft, you feel it hard to imagine, what it means to live behind barbed wire – it is always difficult to imagine things that one has not experienced oneself. But perhaps you will sympathize with one who has not only to bear the general mental pressure that internment entails, but also has been left without any news from his family for weeks and weeks.

I wish I could express in words more adequately the awkward feeling I have in writing to you in private matters such as these, and especially to a man, whose time is occupied with the public affairs of this country so indefinitely [*sic*] more important than my feelings. But believe me I would not have done it if I had found any other means of getting out of this difficulty. Will you, therefore, accept my apologies for all this.

Yours sincerely

10) Copy of draft letter from Lord Croft to Home Office, dated 27 January (but date struck out), in fact written late June 1940

You will remember that I told you in confidence some months ago that my daughter, Diana, had married a German Jew refugee, and that, although I was distressed at this union, in view of Anglo-German relations, which might lead to complications if war came, I had no reason to think that my son-in-law was other than violently anti-Hitler and well-affected to this country.

This refugee, Manfred Uhlman was, I understand, in the category of those regarded as safe. My daughter, Diana Uhlman, is expecting to be confined about July 1st and is staying with my sister, Mrs. Baird of Reeves Green, Wareside, Ware, prior to her confinement in a local hospital.

Manfred Uhlman had special permission from the Chief Constable of Herts, Bow Street and the Hampstead police (he resides in Hampstead) to visit his wife in the peculiar circumstances. He was preparing to return to London by the 8.47 train from Mardocks, having duly reported to the Ware police station the day before, when at 7.45 a.m. the Ware police called to take him to an internment camp.

Would you kindly let me know if this internment is general for German nationals in this category, or whether this action was taken in error owing to some round-up in Hertfordshire, where Manfred Uhlman had received special permission for a temporary visit to his wife about to be confined, also whether M. Uhlman's case will go before a Tribunal?

If the internment is general I have no comment to make but if his case was exceptional *without grave cause for suspicion,* I submit that the arrest for internment was harsh and a very cruel shock to my daughter in the special circumstances, and difficult to justify in view of his special leave granted by the police concerned.

I would be grateful if I might have an early reply as my daughter's health is not unnaturally affected and I would like to give her the definite decision one way or another.

I need hardly say that I approve of the strongest action by the Home Office in seeking the security of the State and ask for this information not as a father but as a citizen concerned lest there be a miscarriage of justice.

11) Osbert Peake, Home Office, to Lord Croft, 26 July 1940

Dear Croft,

Thank you for your letter of July 24th.

We are still proceeding with applications from British-born women to recover British nationality under the provisions of Section 10 (6) of the British Nationality and Status of Aliens Act, 1914, as amended, where the husband was placed in Category C, notwithstanding the fact that he may now be interned. In these circumstances, there is no objection in principle to the completion of your daughter's application, and I am making enquiries to see exactly how it stands.

Arrangements have now been made to ensure that no internee who has a British-born wife will be sent overseas unless his wife is willing to accompany him. You may safely, therefore, give your daughter the assurance in this matter that she is so anxious to have.

Yours sincerely
Osbert Peake

NOTES

Letters in possession of the Imperial War Museum [DDF, IWM, 78/19/1]; original in Uhlman estate.

1. Heinz: Heinz Worner (1910–), sculptor, whom Uhlman knew through the Free German League of Culture, had emigrated via Prague to England in 1939 and was deported to Canada in 1940. The identity of 'Hans' is uncertain.
2. Diana and Fred's fourth wedding anniversary.
3. Richard Carline, 'The Dating and Provenance of Negro Art', in *The Burlington Magazine*, October 1940, pp.115–23. Richard Carline (1896–1980), artist, friend of Uhlman. The article included ten photographs of African sculpture of which three bear the name of Fred Uhlman as owner.

Figure 10. *Untitled*. View over Hutchinson Square, 1940.
Reproduced by kind permission of the IWM.

Figure 11. *Untitled*. Child in a fantastic landscape, from 'A mon enfant nouveau né' series, 1940.
Reproduced by kind permission of the IWM.

Figure 12. *Untitled.* Girl with balloon and gallows, 1940.
Reproduced by kind permission of the IWM.

Figure 13. *Untitled.* Child with balloon among ruined buildings, 1940.
Reproduced by kind permission of the BM.

Figure 14. *Untitled.* War fantasy with crucified Christ, 1940.
Reproduced by kind permission of the BM.

Figure 15. *Untitled.* Child hanging from a gallows, 1940.
Reproduced by kind permission of the BM.

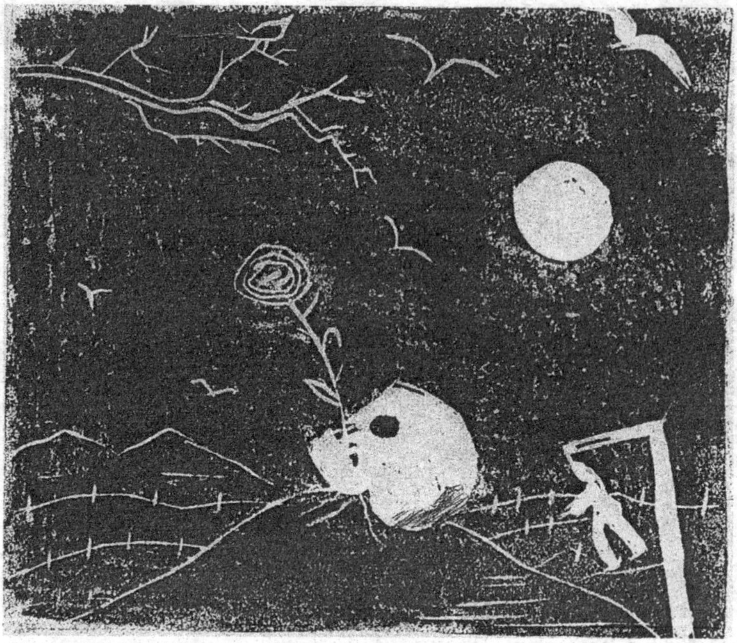

Figure 16. *Untitled.* Skull, flowers, gallows, 1940.
Reproduced by kind permission of the IWM.

Figure 17. *Das Totenschiff – The Ship of the Dead,* 'Internment series', 1940.
Reproduced by kind permission of the IWM.

Figure 18. *Untitled.* Boat and rowers, 1940. Linocut.
Reproduced by kind permission of the IWM.

Figure 19. *Untitled.* Dance of Death, 1940.
Reproduced by kind permission of the BM.

Figure 20. *Little Girl with War Criminals*, 1940.
Reproduced by kind permission of the Fred Uhlman estate.

Figure 21. *Untitled*. From 'Ecclesia Militans' series. Four monks in flight, 1940.
Reproduced by kind permission of the BM.

Figure 22. *Clothing Caught on a Branch and Lying in a Field*, 'Internment series', 1940. Reproduced by kind permission of the IWM.

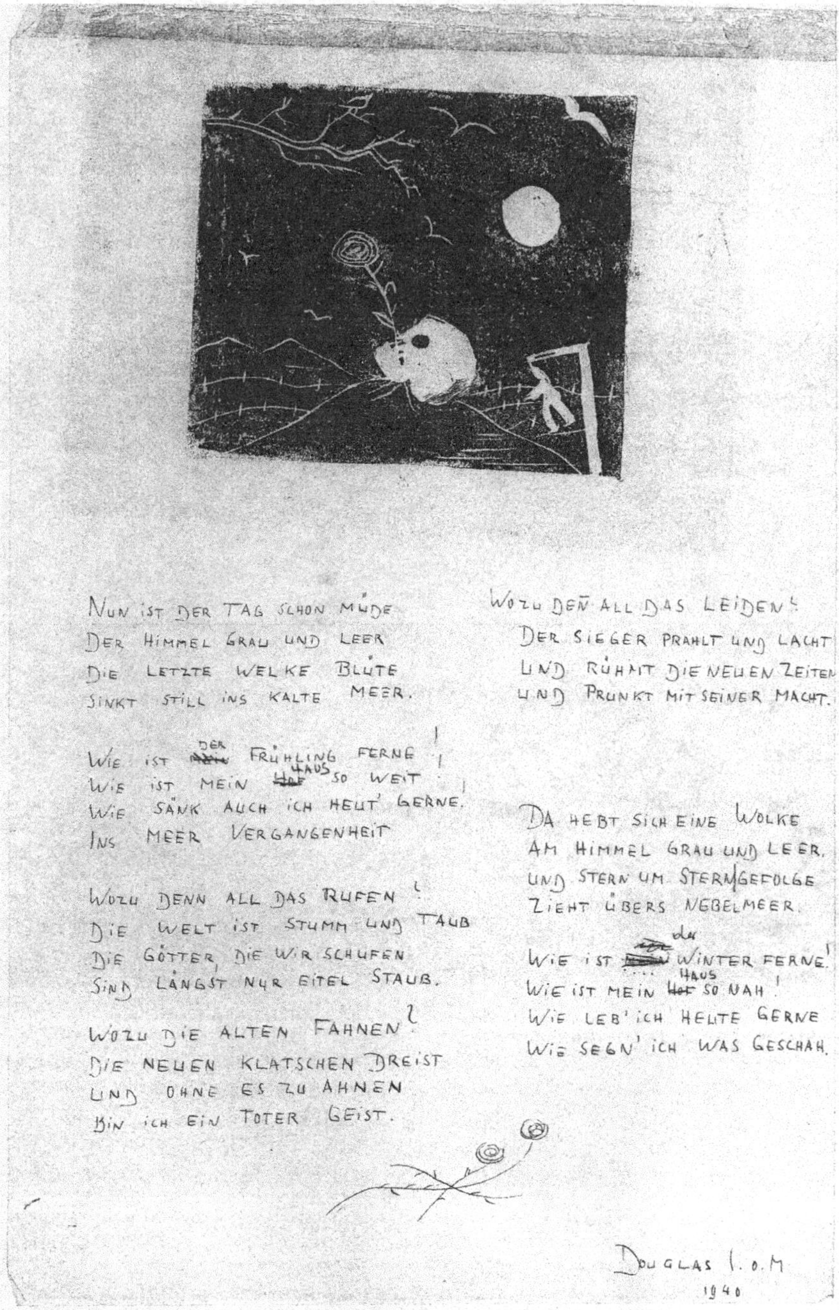

Nun ist der Tag schon müde
Der Himmel grau und leer
Die letzte welke Blüte
Sinkt still ins kalte Meer.

Wie ist der Frühling ferne!
Wie ist mein Haus so weit!
Wie sänk auch ich heut' gerne!
Ins Meer Vergangenheit

Wozu denn all das Rufen?
Die Welt ist stumm und taub
Die Götter, die wir schufen
Sind längst nur eitel Staub.

Wozu die alten Fahnen?
Die neuen klatschen dreist
Und ohne es zu ahnen
Bin ich ein toter Geist.

Wozu deñ all das Leiden?
Der Sieger prahlt und lacht
Und rühmt die neuen Zeiten
Und prunkt mit seiner Macht.

Da hebt sich eine Wolke
Am Himmel grau und leer.
Und Stern um Sterngefolge
Zieht übers Nebelmeer.

Wie ist der Winter ferne!
Wie ist mein Haus so nah!
Wie leb' ich heute gerne
Wie segn' ich was geschah.

Douglas I.o.M
1940

Figure 23. Uhlman poem and untitled linocut of skull and gallows, 1940.
Reproduced by kind permission of the IWM.

PART III

7. *Internment and Autobiography*

Charmian Brinson and Anna Müller-Härlin

Fred Uhlman, in fact, wrote three different accounts of his internment (of which two – the first and the third – are reproduced in the present volume). The first one was written actually on the Isle of Man in 1940; the subsequent two were written largely from memory decades later. While the first was a private diary, written only for himself, the second and third were composed for a public audience with the aim of sharing the internment experience. These two later accounts form part of Uhlman's continuous engagement, from the 1960s onwards, in writing both autobiographical as well as fictional work.[1] He had always enjoyed writing and, at a time when his success as a painter was waning, this alternative occupation now intensified.

In Hutchinson Camp, Uhlman wrote a diary in German, which he later entitled 'H.M. Loyal Internee'.[2] Twenty years later, in 1960, he devoted Chapter Sixteen of his autobiography, *The Making of an Englishman*, to his experiences at Ascot and on the Isle of Man.[3] Then, in 1979, almost forty years after his internment, Uhlman felt that, in addition to the chapter, his original German diary could be of interest to a broader readership. He translated and embellished his diary with later recollections, added an introduction and postscript, entitled it 'The Story of *Captivity*' (with reference to his 1946 volume of internment drawings)[4] and hoped that one day it would be published.[5] This was the reason that he donated a copy to the

Imperial War Museum. The 1979 memoir and the chapter from *The Making of an Englishman* bear strong similarities in tone to one another: both are in general more lighthearted than his 1940 diary and have a strong anecdotal vein. From them the reader gains an insight into how Uhlman wanted his internment to be remembered, on the one hand, but also how memory can become distorted with the passage of time on the other (as will be discussed below).

As we have seen, the 1940 diary constitutes an impressive and touching document both of the artistic community and its activities in Hutchinson Camp and of Uhlman's feelings of depression, as well as of how the experience of internment crucially influenced his own artistic output at the time. Written in very small and sometimes illegible handwriting, it consists in total of nineteen pages, commencing with his day of arrest in June. It unexpectedly breaks off after a description of the first, rather unpleasant night at Ascot, starting again in September and continuing until the day of his release.[6] Uhlman meticulously recorded the lectures he attended, noting the lecturer's name as well as the topic and often adding a small summary of the talk. Concerts he heard are referred to, as are conversations he had with various fellow internees. He listed which books he was reading, when he did not feel too depressed to read, and included a number of poems he had written himself. He also regularly recorded his anxious wait for mail from his wife Diana as well as for post relating to the possible expediting of his release.

The diary represents, in fact, a watershed in Uhlman's use of his mother tongue. After the war, he would abandon German as his first language, even – generally speaking – in letter writing,[7] considering it irrevocably linked to the horrors of the Third Reich. Indeed, the German language represented not only the Nazi regime to him, it was also painfully related to his own German memories.[8]

The 1979 memoir is introduced by Uhlman himself as the English translation of his original diary. However, it actually constitutes a very different version of the text. In the 1979 document, facts, fiction and memories have been fused. Not only have whole days been added from memory, but passages from the earlier text have deliberately been omitted or altered. Often the changes that Uhlman has made to his text are small while also being meaningful. For example, a party he gave celebrating his daughter's three-month birthday turns from a 'tiring birthday celebration' into a 'marvellous birthday party' (3 October). In addition he often tended to exaggerate, asserting, for instance, in the introduction to the 1979 memoir that he founded the Free German League of Culture, an organization that he in fact co-founded with others.

As for the general mood of both documents, the overwhelming depression that features so strongly in the diary is emphasized in the later memoir, too, with Uhlman stressing in his introduction that internment had represented a 'traumatic experience'. Yet there is a marked difference in tone and perspective from one to the other. While the original German-language diary concerns itself primarily with Uhlman's current state of mind, the later memoir places particular emphasis on his internment acquaintances and also comments on life in general. In the postscript, he resumes almost nostalgically: 'What luck I then had to have been a member of one of the finest universities I have ever attended.'

In the memoir, Uhlman also focuses on the anecdotal potential of internment, writing for example at length on the Dada artist Kurt Schwitters (1887–1948). In the original German diary, on the other hand, Schwitters' name only crops up occasionally. It is true that Uhlman knew Schwitters during their internment – like him, Schwitters was a regular visitor at the artists' café and was involved in the artists' activities in the camp. In addition, Uhlman spent time in Schwitters' room having his portrait painted by him.[9] However, they were far from being close friends at the time. Admittedly Uhlman never explicitly suggested that this was the case; but it seems that it was the attraction of Schwitters' later fame that caused Uhlman to write at such length on their acquaintance in the 1979 memoir.

Uhlman's recollections of Kurt Schwitters as well as of the busy cultural programme also feature large in the chapter that portrays the internment experience in Uhlman's autobiography, *The Making of an Englishman;* indeed he asserts that 'the memory of all these men in pursuit of knowledge is one of the most moving and encouraging that I brought back from the strange microcosm in which I lived for so many months'.[10] Apart from his internment, Uhlman concentrates on his childhood in Stuttgart, his school days, the impact of the First World War and the 1918 German Revolution, his years as a student and his career as a lawyer, with the flight to France, then to Spain and later to the United Kingdom forming a slightly smaller section. The autobiography concludes with the end of the Second World War. Since its first publication, the *Englishman* has long been out of print in England.[11] Nevertheless, because of its often entertaining quality, Uhlman's autobiography has established itself as a popular source in the literature on exile in Great Britain. Reference to Uhlman's autobiography is not generally made, however, in order to consider his work as an artist and a painter, but rather to emphasize or illustrate particular aspects of refugee life.[12]

Interestingly, it is the chapter on internment which has received the greatest attention. The passage on the dilemma of choosing between coinciding lectures – of Chinese Theatre versus Byzantine Music, and so on[13] – that was quoted in Chapter Two of this study, is frequently cited in connection with the impressive list of people interned on the Isle of Man and the speedily organized cultural programme. However, contrary to this description, the lectures did not in fact overlap.[14] While Uhlman simply embellished in order to illustrate the rich variety of cultural activities on offer in the camp, readers often assume that this passage describes a predicament with which the internees had to contend on a daily basis.

In fact, neither the Internment Diary nor the Internment Memoir nor, for that matter, the autobiography can offer the reader an accurate account of Uhlman's experiences in Hutchinson Camp, their value lying rather in the fact that all three are documents to be read as texts and then deconstructed. What they do reveal is how Uhlman, as an older man, wished to remember his internment as well as what he intended to convey to his readership. To explore the omissions and gaps in the memoir as compared to the diary, as above, can be rewarding in as much as they indicate a shift in emphasis. Rather than simply establishing that the diary, memoir and autobiography contain inaccuracies – which they of course do – it is perhaps more instructive to ask why Uhlman would have chosen to make such changes. For an author used to working with both fiction and documentary genres, it may furthermore have been a matter of him no longer being able to distinguish between what actually took place and the memories of internment, as recounted many times over in social and public situations. Cultural historian Aleida Assmann distinguishes between three types of memory – personal, collective and cultural – which can at times coexist, overlap and shape the way in which a person remembers events. Indeed, Uhlman's personal memory and the collective memory of internment may well have become enmeshed to the point where differentiation has become impossible. Assmann defines remembrance as 'singular and disparate acts of reconstructing and reclaiming individual experiences'.[15] Remembering events later in life is therefore not a question of listing facts but rather of sharing what makes sense in terms of the person one has become and of the aspects one wants to emphasize.

In fact, Uhlman's autobiography can be seen to have formed the prelude to an ongoing occupation of his to write down his life for a public readership. Of this project, the 1979 Internment Memoir forms one part. Uhlman's wish to be remembered after his death also led him to be engaged from 1965 until his death in 1985 in writing what he named the 'Journal of a Painter'. From 1974, Uhlman started to donate the 'Journal', consisting of seven volumes, to the British Library;[16] six volumes are today located in the British Library,[17] and one in the artist's estate. Uhlman, who wished the volumes to be published after the deaths of himself and his wife,[18] intended the 'Journal' to be a memoir as well as a supplement to *The Making of an Englishman*. While the first two volumes exhibit a clear structure, summarizing reminiscences and opinions in chapter-like form, Volumes III and IV repeat many pre-1945 events. The last three volumes, written between 1981 and 1985, begin to take on the form of a diary, with almost daily entries. However, Uhlman's 'Journal of a Painter' fails as an entirely convincing complementary work to his autobiography. Set out in the form of memoirs, often produced on the basis of former diaries which he then destroyed, the 'Journal' loses its authenticity as a primary source for facts and dates for pre-1968 events. It does, however, offer an insight into Uhlman's state of mind, indicating how there remained in him, decades after his emigration, a feeling of uprootedness and an ongoing struggle to come to terms with his past. It presents us with a detailed picture both of Uhlman as an elderly man and of how he perceived himself within British society.

In this connection, it is perhaps noteworthy that the experience of exile has triggered a large number of autobiographical texts, both published and unpublished. While professional writers have felt the urge to share their experiences, people who had never written before, from all sorts of career and social backgrounds, were equally driven to record their fate.[19] Having examined autobiographical texts by women refugees from Nazism who fled to England, one of the present writers has come to the conclusion that, despite the diversity of memoirs, similarities in themes and circumstances are sufficiently remarkable for it to be possible to speak in terms of a 'collective autobiography'.[20] Although these particular observations referred to texts by female refugees only, the concept of a 'collective autobiography' can probably also be applied to exile autobiographies in general. For although individual fates undoubtedly differed greatly (with Uhlman's conversion from lawyer to painter certainly not constituting an average exile experience, for example), many of the coordinates of exile are identical in such documents. The experience of internment would be one obvious example, another would be the culture shock of having to come to terms with living amongst the English. Common threads in these autobiographical texts are the wish to recall a childhood and youth spent in Germany or Austria; the flight from Hitler; and the difficult processes of assimilation and acculturation. The urge to record the experience of exile was frequently driven by the author's conviction that he or she was representative of the time[21] – which was also one of the reasons why Uhlman came to write an autobiography.[22]

In addition, in reporting on his individual fate, Uhlman demonstrated his longing to be remembered posthumously. He was, as has already been mentioned, anxious that he would be forgotten – 'I shall hardly be remembered a few weeks after my death', so he asserts in *The Making of an Englishman*[23] – yet at the same time he was comforted by the thought that in his autobiography, which he saw as a document of 'an average man and his time',[24] he might have achieved something of lasting value. Moreover, Uhlman's obsession with writing about himself in the last decades of his life might also be described as an attempt to unify a discontinuous life.[25] By looking into the past, by narrating and remembering his former life in Germany, a continuity was established with his new life in exile. The desire to look back at his life as 'fulfilled', to view it as a life which, despite its discontinuities of place, friends, family and language, was 'worthwhile', is strongly expressed in *The Making of an Englishman*, in the 1979 internment memoir and in the 'Journal of a Painter'.

* * * * *

In his groundbreaking work from 1984 on literary production in the internment camps, Michael Seyfert analyses and categorizes the texts that emerged in these unusual conditions: on the whole, he contends, the situation was scarcely conducive to the production of full-length literary works; and such extended texts as were completed there, like Heinrich Fraenkel's *Help Us Germans to Beat the Nazis!*, 1941, tended to be of a journalistic, political or academic nature.[26] Generally speaking, then, the texts that emerged from the internment camps were conceived and executed on a much smaller scale: sketches, essays, letters, songs, poetry and diaries (with Uhlman, as we have seen, incorporating into his diary some of the poetry that he wrote on a semi-regular basis while in internment). Seyfert points to the extreme pathos that characterizes many of these works – a response whose intensity is possibly disproportionate even given the undoubted hardships experienced – explaining it as a symptom of 'two-fold nostalgia', that is a longing for the normality of the time before persecution and emigration, coupled with a desire for a return at least to the 'normality' of life in emigration, prior to internment.[27] Livia Laurent, another chronicler of the internment experience, who, like Uhlman, interspersed the prose text of her semi-fictional/semi-autobiographical *A Tale of Internment* with occasional poems, made use of the expression 'the exile of internment', suggesting perhaps that internment represented a second or twofold exile for her, an exile within exile.[28] Interned authors, as Seyfert notes, have themselves later tended to account for the high level of emotion that pervades many of the writings produced in internment as a product of 'barbed wire sickness', of captivity.[29]

In this connection, it is perhaps of some interest to consider Uhlman's Internment Diary alongside those of two further internees, Austrians as it happens, the author Robert Neumann[30] and the composer and musicologist Hans Gál.[31] There are, of course, a number of basic differences to be noted here: for a start the three men were in different camps (Neumann was held in Huyton and Mooragh, Gál in Central Promenade Camp) and were interned for varying periods of time (with Neumann being released in late August, and Gál in September, both several months before Uhlman). What these three diaries have in common, however, is that at the time of writing none of them was intended for publication but rather constituted a private means of recording and confronting events and feelings; and that they covered the entire internment experience, from arrest to release, though in varying degrees of detail (undoubtedly the physical circumstances of the internment camps rendered sustained concentration difficult). Neumann, like Uhlman, uses his diary, in which, as Richard Dove has observed, 'the words "despair" or "despairing" are a leitmotif',[32] to record his feelings of frustration and depression. The causes for the two men's desperation, such as lack of news from the outside world and impotence in the face of force majeure, appear strikingly similar if not identical. Uhlman anxiously awaits news of his wife and new born baby, for instance; Neumann, who has heard news of the impending internment of Category 'B' women, fears that his life partner, Rolly Becker, will likewise be interned (as she indeed soon is).

A further similarity consists in the fact that, at much the same time, that is around twenty years after the event, both Uhlman and Neumann chose to revisit and recast their internment experiences for publication, Uhlman for his English-language autobiography *The Making of An Englishman,* and Neumann for his German-language book of memoirs, *Ein leichtes Leben.*[33] While using incidents recorded in their respective diaries as a basis, both authors then proceeded to distance themselves from the events in question by use of irony and exaggeration and essentially to semi-fictionalize the whole experience, the tone of both accounts being not too far removed from that of Richard Friedenthal's novel, *Die Welt in der Nussschale,* which is indubitably a *fictional* representation of life in Hutchinson Camp, even if with biographical elements.[34]

Hans Gál's diary, on the other hand, has enjoyed a rather different publication history, being published only in 2003 and by Gál's daughter rather than by Gál himself. It was, so Eva Fox-Gál recounts in her introduction to her father's published diary, never intended for publication, indeed the manuscript bore instructions to that effect on its title page. Unlike both Uhlman and Neumann, during his lifetime Gál was distinctly unwilling to speak of his internment, partly – according to his daughter once again – because a critical statement might have smacked of disloyalty towards his adopted country, partly because of a reluctance to expose feelings on the subject which were deeply painful.[35] While it is evident that Gál must have reworked the text before entrusting it to his daughter,[36] in tone and subject matter the published text has retained a painful rawness (and in more senses than one, for Gál's internment was marked for him by a lengthy attack of agonizing eczema).

Yet, despite the physical pain and the desperate anxieties for himself and his family (*inter alia* for his son Franz whom he – incorrectly

– feared to have been on the ill-fated *Arandora Star*), Gál was able to lose himself in his work, in musical composition and performance, in a way that neither Uhlman the artist nor Neumann the writer could manage. In fact, having thrown himself wholeheartedly into rehearsals for the Central Promenade Camp revue, *What a Life!*, Gál even elected to postpone his release date by a day in order not to miss the performance.[37] It is probably not going too far to claim that Gál's diary testifies to the transcending of physical and mental suffering through art in a way that most other internment diaries do not.

The three diaries considered here may be considered as exemplary of their kind. Each originating from an author of some eminence in the exile community and beyond, the diaries themselves (or at least texts based on the diaries) have been accepted for publication in a way that other similar texts by less well-known authors have not. There are undoubtedly other internment diaries of a greater or lesser degree of completion lying in attics or bottom drawers whose significance has not (or not yet) been recognized and which remain unpublished. To take one example, the fragmentary diary of the singer Johanna Metzger-Lichtenstern,[38] who was interned in the Rushen Women's Camp, is of interest in the present connection, *inter alia* because of some distinct similarities in tone with that of Hans Gál. Certainly in Metzger-Lichtenstern's case, as in that of the other internees, there were anxieties and losses (she had only very recently married and was upset at being separated from her husband). She, however, like Gál, threw herself into music making with other likeminded internees to such an extent that not infrequently, as she notes in her diary, she lacked even the time to write to her family. For Metzger-Lichtenstern – and in this she goes some way beyond Gál – internment turned out to be a time of great personal and artistic development that largely compensated her for the hardship and loss of liberty endured.[39] It may be that, following on from the (admittedly loose) concept of 'collective exile autobiography' that was mentioned earlier, it is possible to think in terms of a 'collective internment account' in which the same sequence of events, the same emotions, fears and privations occur and reoccur over the same relatively short time span but in which responses to the situation may vary greatly.

The authors of this volume have taken the decision, contrary to Uhlman's own intentions but in consultation with the Uhlman family, to publish both of Uhlman's previously unpublished internment accounts – his 1940 Diary as well as his 1979 Memoir – as being of equal interest to today's reader, indeed as complementary one to another, with the feelings of outrage and bitterness expressed in the earlier document being presented in a rather different perspective years later. If, in 1979, internment appeared to Fred Uhlman to be less daunting than during his time as an 'enemy alien', this does not render the memoir any less valuable.

And finally, Uhlman's Diary and later Memoir are of particular interest to scholars and general readers in that these accounts constitute a highly uncommon source on a painter interned. The former internee and art historian Klaus Hinrichsen, it is true, has written in detail on the artistic activities in Hutchinson Camp,[40] but none of Uhlman's fellow painters has published on the issue. Uhlman's accounts of his internment provide us not only with a view of life in Hutchinson Camp and of the workings of the artists' community within it, but also an insight into an artist in captivity. In Uhlman's case, the autobiographical writings on internment can be seen, therefore, as complementary to his drawings and linocuts of that same time, a time of great doubt and despair but also one of heightened personal and artistic sensibilities.

NOTES

1. It is not the aim of this chapter to discuss Uhlman's fictional writings; however it should at least be noted here that his best known fictional publication, the novella *Reunion* (1971), a story set in Stuttgart in 1932 with the rise of Nazism as its backdrop, though not autobiographical, draws on specific occurrences in Uhlman's own boyhood and youth.
2. Fred Uhlman, 'HM Loyal Internee', unpublished manuscript, 1940, Fred Uhlman Estate.
3. Fred Uhlman, *The Making of an Englishman* (London: Gollancz, 1960).
4. Fred Uhlman, *Captivity: Twenty-four Drawings by Fred Uhlman* (London: Jonathan Cape, 1946).
5. Unpublished typescript, 1979, Fred Uhlman Estate.
6. Unfortunately, the pages between July and September have been lost.
7. He did make a few exceptions. For example, he communicated in German with his two oldest friends from Stuttgart, and he also corresponded in German with Paul Westheim (in all three cases the use of English would have posed a language barrier).
8. Uhlman's ambiguous feelings towards the German language were not exceptional amongst German-speaking exiles (on this, see also Marian Malet and Anthony Grenville (eds), *Changing Countries* (London: Libris, 2002). While Uhlman never wrote in German again, apart from in occasional letters, his attitude to his mother tongue underwent a change in the mid-1970s when he was seemingly overwhelmed by a longing for the language he had for so many years suppressed. He wrote at this time: 'After nearly twenty years I read German poetry – which I have always loved in contrast to German prose – again and I was overwhelmed by its infinite beauty and made miserable by the total impossibility to translate it,' Fred Uhlman, 'Journal of a Painter', IV (1976–78), British Library, London, ADD 74738, n. p.

9. Kurt Schwitters, *Portrait of Fred Uhlman*, 1940, oil on board, 102 x 75 cm, Hatton Gallery, Newcastle upon Tyne.
10. Uhlman, *The Making of an Englishman*, p.233.
11. Today it is available in French, German, Italian, Dutch and Catalan, however.
12. For example in Daniel Snowman's study of the cultural impact on Britain of refugees from Nazism, Uhlman's autobiography is used as an established source, while his biography itself is not examined. Snowman quotes at length from *The Making of an Englishman* (and also to some extent from *Reunion*) in order to illustrate the fate of refugees; Uhlman is introduced as an 'artist and writer', but the reader learns nothing about his career as such (see Daniel Snowman, *The Hitler Emigrés: The Cultural Impact on Britain of Refugees from Nazism* (London: Chatto and Windus, 2002)).
13. Uhlman, *The Making of an Englishman*, pp.232 f.
14. Klaus Hinrichsen, the head of the Cultural Department at Hutchinson Camp, recalled: 'We spent hours making sure that no two important lectures would take place simultaneously – it was a very complicated jigsaw aligning times and venues and had to be done weeks in advance' (letter from Hinrichsen to Anna Müller-Härlin, 15 July 2003).
15. Aleida Assmann, 'Zwischen Geschichte und Gedächtnis', in *Geschichtsvergessenheit, Geschichtsversessenheit: vom Umgang mit deutschen Vergangenheiten nach 1945* (Stuttgart: Deutsche Verlags-Anstalt, 1999), p.27.
16. Letter from Daniel Waley, Department of Manuscripts, British Library, to Uhlman, 18 February 1974, Fred Uhlman Estate.
17. Fred Uhlman, 'Journal of a Painter', British Library, ADD 74735-74740.
18. Letter from Uhlman to Waley, 9 April 1985, Fred Uhlman Estate.
19. Richard Critchfield, 'Einige Überlegungen zur Problematik der Exilautobiographik', in Thomas Koebner, Wolf Köpke and Joachim Radkau (eds), *Exilforschung: Erinnerungen ans Exil – kritische Lektüre der Autobiographien nach 1933 und andere Themen*, 21 (1984), p.41. For exile autobiographies written in German, see Ingrid Hannich-Bode, 'Autobiographien aus dem Exil', in Claus-Dieter Krohn, Erwin Rotermund *et al.* (eds), *Exilforschung: Rückblick und Perspektiven*, 14 (1996), pp.200 ff. For a list containing autobiographies written in English see Waltraud Strickhausen, 'Auswahlbibliographie englischsprachiger Publikationen deutscher und österreichischer Exilschriftsteller in Großbritannien', in Dieter Sevin (ed.), *Die Resonanz des Exils: Gelungene und misslungene Rezeption deutschsprachiger Exilautoren* (Amsterdam: Rodopi, 1992), pp.383 ff. (which includes Uhlman's work). On women exile writers see Charmian Brinson, 'Autobiography in exile: The reflections of women refugees from Nazism in British exile', in J.M. Ritchie (ed.), *Yearbook of the Research Centre for German and Austrian Exile Studies: German-speaking Exiles in Great Britain*, 3 (2001), pp.1–21.
20. Brinson, 'Autobiography in Exile', p.4.
21. Critchfield, 'Einige Überlegungen zur Problematik der Exilautobiographik', p.49.
22. Uhlman, *The Making of an Englishman*, p.252.
23. Ibid., p.251.
24. Uhlman, *The Making of an Englishman*, p.252.
25. Elisabeth Bronfen, 'Exil in der Literatur: Zwischen Metapher und Realität', in *arcadia: Zeitschrift für vergleichende Literaturwissenschaft*, 28, 2 (1993), p.170.
26. Michael Seyfert, *Im Niemandsland: Deutsche Exilliteratur in britischer Internierung: Ein unbekanntes Kapitel der Kulturgeschichte des Zweiten Weltkriegs* (Berlin: Das Arsenal, 1984), p.67. In any case, as mentioned in Chapter Two above, Fraenkel had official British backing for his book and was granted appropriate conditions in which to write it.
27. Seyfert, *Im Niemandsland*, p.71.
28. Livia Laurent, *A Tale of Internment* (London: George Allen and Unwin, 1942), p.8.
29. Seyfert, *In Niemandsland*, p.71.
30. Neumann's unpublished 123-page internment diary is held in the Neumann Papers, Österreichische Nationalbibliothek, ser.n.21.608 (I am endebted to Richard Dove for this information).
31. Hans Gál, *Musik hinter Stacheldraht: Tagebuchblätter aus dem Sommer 1940* (Berne/Berlin etc.: Peter Lang, 2003).
32. Richard Dove, 'KZ auf Englisch: Robert Neumann's Internment Diary', in Charmian Brinson, Richard Dove, Marian Malet and Jennifer Taylor (eds), *'England? Aber wo liegt es?'*

Deutsche und österreichische Emigranten in Großbritannien, 1933–1945 (Munich: iudicium, 1996), p.159.

33. Robert Neumann, *Ein leichtes Leben: Bericht über mich selbst und Zeitgenossen* (Vienna/Munich/Basle: Desch, 1963).
34. On this, see also Chapter Two, above.
35. Eva Fox-Gál, 'Einleitung I' in Gál, *Musik hinter Stacheldraht.*, p.xviii.
36. The original diary entries are no longer extant, however.
37. This was not a unique occurrence: the renowned educationalist Minna Specht, who was in charge of educational provision in the Rushen Women's Camp (which also housed a number of children), also declined to leave her work in Rushen when her release date came through.
38. Diary in private possession of Johanna Metzger-Lichtenstern, London.
39. On Johanna Metzger-Lichtenstern in internment, see Charmian Brinson, '"Keine verlorene Zeit": Musik im britischen Fraueninternierungslager Rushen', in Anna-Christine Rhode-Jüchtern and Maria Kublitz-Kramer (eds), *Echolos: Klangwelten verfolgter Musikerinnen in der NS-Zeit* (Bielefeld: Aisthesis-Verlag, 2004), pp.243–4.
40. See for example, 'Visual Art behind the Wire', in David Cesarani and Tony Kushner (eds), *The Internment of Aliens in Twentieth-Century Britain* (London: Frank Cass, 1993).

8. 'Should the artist portray his age?'[1] Reflections on Fred Uhlman's Internment Art Works

Julia Winckler

Looking back at his artistic output towards the end of his life, Fred Uhlman described the art works produced during six months of captivity, which saw him first interned in Ascot, then in Hutchinson Camp, Douglas, Isle of Man as 'the best thing' he had ever done: 'They kept pouring out of me like a river and they kept me sane.'[2] Despite a deep and growing depression, Uhlman produced on average one drawing a day, resulting in between 150–200 in total,[3] participated in cultural activities, kept an internment diary, and wrote poems, which he illustrated with linocuts for his wife Diana.[4] This artistic engagement and the connections he made with other artists in the camp were vital to Uhlman in making the internment experience more bearable.

A study of Uhlman's art work within the context of exile gives insight into how Uhlman was affected by his captivity and how he explored this experience artistically. This chapter will concentrate on a small number of internment drawings and linocuts held at the Imperial War Museum, London, which can be seen as representative of Uhlman's overall internment art production.

Several kinds of writing exist on internment art, and on Uhlman's art work in particular. There are commentaries by former internees who knew Uhlman personally, some written during or shortly after the war,[5] some many years later.[6] In recent years, a rapidly growing body of literature and in-depth studies on the British internment experience have emerged, mainly within the fields of German and Austrian exile studies and art history. One of the first, and most thorough books to examine the cultural and artistic life of internees in Britain is Michael Seyfert's *Im Niemandsland*;[7] Seyfert and others consider how the creative expression of refugees (as evidenced in the production of camp newspapers, personal diaries, letters, discussion groups, poetry, theatre and cabaret performances as well as the creation of art works and exhibitions) was affected by the experience of exile. He explores themes and functions, including the therapeutic aspects of creative production.[8]

Moreover, scholars working within the field of art history have examined the contributions that exiled artists have made to British culture, and to British art in particular. The 1986 exhibition 'Art in Exile in Great Britain 1933–45' at the Camden Arts Centre remains the most comprehensive exhibition in Britain to date, providing an overview of the significant contributions exiled artists have made to British life. In recent years art historians have become increasingly interested in exploring the impact of the internment experience itself on artistic output. While Jutta Vinzent explores the possibility that the circumstances of internment led to the development of a particular aesthetic of internment art, Rosamunde Neugebauer emphasizes the ongoing influence of artistic traditions and themes in addition to the role the experience of exile had on interned artists.[9] In Fred Uhlman's case, it was in exile that his artistic interests developed and he took up painting as a profession. It was in internment that he expressed his experiences and uncertainties by drawing on Christian iconography, as well as developing his own personal iconography: most notably the girl and balloon sequence.

It must be noted that Uhlman's art works did not receive the kind of attention he might have wished for. Much to Fred Uhlman's personal disappointment, his only book of internment drawings, *Captivity*, which was published in 1946, failed to become a commercial success, and his biggest regret in life, as he states in his autobiography *The Making of an Englishman*, was that his ambition to become a great painter never materialized.[10] In her 2004 doctoral thesis on the life and work of Fred Uhlman, the art historian Anna Müller-Härlin devotes a chapter to Uhlman's internment art, concluding that 'Uhlman succeeded brilliantly in conveying uncanny visions of a destroyed world' and that his works can be seen as 'powerful indicators of his emotional and creative experiences during internment'.[11]

INTERNMENT AND ARTISTIC PRODUCTION AT ASCOT AND HUTCHINSON SQUARE CAMPS

As an active anti-Nazi, who had left Germany as early as 1933, Uhlman felt depressed at being interned as an 'enemy alien'. Most of the refugee artists also felt marginalized by their arrest and subsequent internment. Art historian Klaus E. Hinrichsen, a fellow internee, later described the artists' double sense of betrayal, first at the hands of their former home country, then by Britain: 'The shared experience of all the artists was the loss of homeland and the internment in their country of refuge [...] the trauma and the sense of loss were too deep to be forgotten.'[12]

All the refugees were deeply preoccupied by the war, many feeling angry and helpless at not being allowed to join the British war effort. They had all recently experienced physical and cultural displacement and had looked to Britain for protection and support. In addition they were deeply worried about relatives left behind in Germany, and about the very real danger that the Battle of Britain could end in Hitler's invasion. In his Internment Diary, Uhlman documented his concerns about the outside world, and civilian life in London: 'What's going on in London? What are people thinking there? Odd how far away we are. How strange! Time doesn't exist for us, we are just counted like cattle.'[13]

For many, captivity led to a complete 'loss of contact with the world outside'.[14] It is therefore not surprising that Uhlman hardly comments on the political situation in Germany; nor does he record any thoughts about his parents or sister who had remained behind.[15] Looking back, former internee Paul Jacobsthal explains that having one's 'space of movement' narrowed represented 'a break in the continuity of existence, an interruption of the normal flux of life, it causes a trauma: the natural relation and proportional importance of present, past and future become distorted'.[16] Each artist's individual experience was different, though, and not all experienced the internment ordeal in the same way.[17] Most felt depressed at having been locked away 'at a time when to be free, to be outside would have been very much greater help to everyone concerned'.[18]

This led to artists debating their function and responsibility in internment. In his diary, Uhlman records a discussion with fellow internees on whether art can ever be non-political, and in particular, on the question of: 'Should the artist portray his age?'[19] Hinrichsen recalls artists debating whether it was 'morally defensible to continue painting flowers and still-life' during wartime and arguing that their work had to represent the times.[20] It has been widely noted that possibly the greatest paradox of internment was the complete artistic freedom enjoyed by the interned artists of Hutchinson Camp. 'Internment created conditions of greater artistic solidarity and opportunity than most of the internees had so far experienced in England.'[21] Hinrichsen points to the irony that while art works created in the camp could 'hardly have been conceived in freedom', the interned artists were asserting, and were granted, their freedom of artistic expression in captivity.[22]

At Ascot the interned artists had not received any support for their artistic abilities. Uhlman recalls an acute shortage of materials there, though the artists became exceptionally inventive in their usage of scarce resources, initially even resorting to using toilet paper for their drawings. However, working conditions improved significantly in Hutchinson Camp. As already mentioned in Chapter Two, above, the artists were helped by Captain H.O. Daniel, who – having realized the exceptional creative skills of the men in his camp – made available makeshift studio space and began to collect the artists' work himself. The first exhibition, which opened on 14 September 1940, gets recorded in Uhlman's Diary as the 'most cheerful day since my internment'.[23]

Initially Uhlman's shared bedroom became his studio: he set up a workspace by placing his suitcase on top of the only two chairs available in the room.[24] Later on in internment he was able to work in the makeshift studio of sculptor Paul Hamann. As already mentioned, all the windows of the houses had been blackened out with blue paint, and the only light bulbs available inside the houses were red (to create a blackout effect). Uhlman recalls working conditions similar to those in a 'fish bowl' during the day time, and a 'brothel' at night.

Diana had ensured that her husband had 'some Indian ink, charcoal, a pen and a block of writing paper'.[25] These materials in particular were of 'enormous importance' to him.[26] While Uhlman completed at least three oil paintings,[27] drawing became his preferred working method. He recalls in his memoir his disinclination to paint: 'Not interested in painting at the moment. Paintings are expressionless, without experience. Only want to draw.'[28]

It is thought that Hellmuth Weissenborn taught Uhlman the technique of lithography.[29] Towards the end of his captivity Uhlman also worked briefly, but intensively, with linocuts. Linoleum was readily available in attics and on the floors of kitchens and corridors, and the artists cut off pieces to make prints, using household utensils instead of linocutters.[30] In addition, linoleum would have offered a relatively easy surface for working, with more precision and a greater variety of effects than engraving into wood. Weissenborn had developed a creative technique using a mangle found in one of the houses to press the inked linoleum plates against paper to make the final linocut prints. Uhlman's linocuts were often reinterpretations of themes and image series already explored in much detail in his internment drawings; the starkness of lines produced through cutting into the linoleum often created a complementary aesthetic. Never having worked in print-making before but almost exclusively in oils, he would have had to learn to anticipate the final positive image from first making a negative image. What appears as a light area in a linocut print is in fact a space where the surface has been reduced or removed, and Uhlman would have had to learn how to pick out which parts of the surface needed to be cut away and which had to be saved.

Detailed information on his brief exploits with sculpture making can be found in his diary as well. The sculptor Paul Hamann started giving lessons – having got hold of some clay – and Uhlman became his pupil in early November: 'Start a small sculpture with Hamann. Bold venture.'[31] Throughout the following week he immersed himself in sculpting, but with disappointing results: 'I am dissatisfied with the sculpture. Much too reminiscent of kitsch.'[32] He described having tried his hand, unsuccessfully, at three different sculptures, resulting in one of them finally getting cast on 30 November. Forty years later, in his Internment Memoir, Uhlman recalls his dissatisfaction, writing with an air of defeatism: 'I am just a painter and nothing else.'[33]

Frequently, Uhlman's creative output was followed by a short period of paralysis. However he was acutely aware of the importance of his work in providing him with a focus. Towards the end of his internment he had 'given up working, a foolish thing to do because work is the only help against the "black desire of the soul"'.[34]

UHLMAN'S MAJOR ARTISTIC THEMES DURING INTERNMENT

In an essay on Uhlman's internment drawings (published elsewhere), Anna Müller-Härlin notes that while various visual references appear in Uhlman's work before and after his internment experience (ruins, black birds, a gateway), themes such as the 'girl and balloon' and the priest series were never taken up again following internment.[35] A close reading of the 1940 Diary reveals that Uhlman produced some of the internment artwork in small sequences. Although he continued to work on the 'girl and balloon' sequence throughout his internment, other visual symbols, including 'the shipwrecked', 'scarecrows' and 'skulls', or the extensive *Ecclesia Militans* sequence, were produced during shorter bursts of creative energy.[36] Different types of production coexisted and at the same time Uhlman also developed visual metaphors in succession. Occasionally diary entries record production dates, which makes it possible to ascertain when Uhlman began or finished an individual drawing or set of drawings. The overall sequencing appears to have been somewhat random, though. More often than not, Uhlman worked on several ideas at the same time, revisiting or abandoning them depending on his mood, the drawing's potential, or the materials available to him that day.

Below, Uhlman's internment art works have been grouped into six major themes, starting with his topographical drawings, which document his experiences first at Ascot, then at Hutchinson internment camps. His second major theme, 'the girl and balloon', was inspired by the birth of his daughter Caroline in July 1940, nine days after his arrest on 25 June. In a third theme Uhlman explores Christian iconography; and a fourth sequence features drawings of ships and shipwrecks. Second to last are memento mori referring to death and transience. The *Ecclesia Militans* series concludes Uhlman's major artistic internment themes.[37]

EXPERIENCES AT ASCOT AND HUTCHINSON CAMPS

Like most interned artists, Uhlman recorded camp life first at Ascot, then at Hutchinson Camp in a realist style. The drawings are descriptive, portraying the physical conditions of camp life: the bunk beds, barbed wire fencing, latrines, watchtowers and fellow internees. However, these topographical drawings are not simply transcriptions of the real, they can be seen as Uhlman's visual articulation of his inner unhappiness. There is a sense of enclosure and suffocation in most of them: menacing dark skies and barbed wire fencing dominate his landscapes. Although initially drawn in clear outlines, Uhlman's scenes become more expressionistic, his mark making more obsessive and layered. In *Ascot* (Figure 8) he drew a row of bunk beds, the lines becoming so heavy as to blacken out entire areas of the page. Instead of an outline drawing, Uhlman was drawing from within: building up mass, applying heavy pen scratching leading to a multitude of dark layered lines. In his Internment Memoir he recalled the shock of seeing the sleeping quarters, 'a large hall with layers and layers of wooden boards, three on top of each other'.[38] In his 1940 Diary, he documented the chaos within the dormitories: 'A long hall containing 90 wooden bunks. In each, three men slept above and three beneath one another [...] by the light of a single candle a few young rabbis were praying [...] I was unable to sleep [...] the gurgling and snoring and whistling and grunting.'[39] Although part of a figurative drawing, the people depicted have been reduced to abstract anonymous shapes, reflecting Uhlman's personal feeling of dehumanization.[40] In another figurative drawing entitled *Ascot – Two Figures Reading by the Fence* (Figure 9), two men are depicted by daunting barbed wire and under a dark, brooding sky, watched over by a camp guard in a threatening looking watchtower.

Uhlman's style and his aesthetic response to his detention progressed after arriving in Hutchinson Camp from Ascot. In Ascot, Uhlman and the other internees had been out of the British public's sight. Hutchinson Camp, on the other hand, was situated right in the centre of Douglas, the Isle of Man's largest town. Although surrounded by barbed wire, Hutchinson Square, with its three and four storey Victorian houses built around a green square and with views of the sea, harbour and nearby hills, was a great improvement over 'beastly' Ascot.[41] However, Uhlman's drawings became even darker here. One of the few exceptions is a linocut print, based on a view over Hutchinson Camp and the nearby sea (*Untitled*, view over Hutchinson Square, Figure 10). Here, Uhlman created an imposing cloud, which hovers above the town like a canopy. In the distance the viewer makes out a small stone fortress and four seagulls floating in the sky. Uhlman referred to seagulls as 'goddesses of the air, who defy gravity and float above the camp'.[42]

Klaus Hinrichsen, interned in Hutchinson himself, explores the survival of German styles and German art in British internment camps in his seminal essay 'Visual Arts Behind the Wire'. He further expands on styles and influences in an interview conducted on behalf of the Imperial War Museum in the late 1970s, when he discusses close to a dozen of the interned artists.[43] Kurt Schwitters, the best-known artist to have been interned in Hutchinson, was still working as a Dadaist there, whereas several of the other artists considered themselves Expressionists and New Realists. Hermann Fechenbach for example was a proponent of New German Realism, whereas the sculptor Georg Ehrlich used a classical style. Paul Hamann had trained with Aristide Maillol and was influenced by German Impressionism. Siegfried Charoux was a Baroque artist, whereas Ernst Müller-Blensdorf drew on late Gothic traditions. Uhlman was surrounded by excellent draftsmen, including Hellmuth Weissenborn who, as Hinrichsen comments, invented the art of engraved windows in the camp. Erich Kahn, an admirer of Oskar Kokoschka, was the greatest painter in the camp in Hinrichsen's view. Many of the artists earned some money painting portraits for fellow internees. Fritz Krämer, a Renaissance style painter, was the most successful portraitist in the camp, whereas Kurt Schwitters charged according to a sliding scale depending on whether a head and shoulder portrait or just a head portrait were asked for.

Despite the broad scope of artistic styles employed by the interned artists, Hinrichsen is of the opinion that artistic development was arrested in most of them rather than that they created groundbreaking new works. This phenomenon may have been due to the fact that 'artists need possibly the cross-fertilization of the countries where they were living'.[44]

Many of the themes explored by the interned artists were based on camp life and everyday experiences. Much of the work was situational with similar iconographies appearing in many of the art works produced in captivity. As Hinrichsen observes, barbed wire was 'integral to the landscape', and several of Uhlman's fellow internees, for example Hermann Fechenbach and Erich Kahn, produced work dominated by barbed wire.[45] Seagulls and the sea were common visual referents deployed by the artists: both became a symbol of freedom. All of the internment camps on the Isle of Man were situated within great proximity of the sea. Seyfert also points out that internees would have been able to observe the sea on a daily basis, leading to the frequent use of the seagull and sea as metaphors to symbolize freedom, and he documents how both featured extensively in the works of interned writers and artists.[46]

While continuing to produce topographical drawings depicting camp life in the square (men playing cards, café scenes), Uhlman also embarked on two original sets of drawings: the first was based thematically on the consequences and horrors of war, and was imbued with a sense of dark foreboding. Drawing on his imagination as well as the particular psychological circumstances, these art works became a way of articulating Uhlman's inner life and fears.

THE GIRL AND BALLOON

The visual referent of a young girl is the most central character featured in Uhlman's work, and appears in a whole series of drawings and linocut prints.[47] In an untitled drawing (*Untitled*, Child in a fantastic landscape, Figure 11) we see her, with her back turned and holding a balloon in her right hand, walking through a valley of death, the latter covered with piled up bodies and open graves. Bodies also hang from gallows, three crosses can be seen in the distance, and vultures fly through the air. Despite finding herself surrounded by death and horror, however, the girl walks 'totally undisturbed, untouchable and triumphant. Death has no dominion over [her]'.[48]

There is both a personal and a deeply political context to these drawings. To Uhlman, the balloon symbolized 'joy and liberty'.[49] It had 'the power to free [the girl] from her disastrous surroundings, because it could float'.[50] Uhlman later explained that these drawings were dedicated 'à mon enfant nouveau né'; the figure of the little girl 'really had to do with my own child who had just been born but who I hadn't even seen then'. 'The child [...] was the future. She was the antithesis to militarism and destruction. She goes marching on and on forever and ever as long as man exists.'[51] The drawing brings to mind the photomontage 'Fascist Memorial' by John Heartfield, where skulls are piled up in the shape of a pyramid.[52] It is likely that Uhlman would have been familiar with, and might have been inspired by, some of Heartfield's political montages, especially since Heartfield had lived with the Uhlmans at 47 Downshire Hill prior to Fred Uhlman's internment (and indeed would continue to live there for several years following Uhlman's release).

In a further linocut (*Untitled*, Girl with balloon and gallows, Figure 12) the little girl reappears in a desolate and brutal landscape, to her left and right dead bodies hang from gallows, a body lies on the ground, barbed wire spreads across the land like a weed, crosses are scattered across the horizon, but in the distance we can make out the sun, and a ray of light moving across the sky. The girl walks on into the distance, seemingly conquering the darkness around her. This brings to mind the myth of the Odyssey in which Odysseus sets off on his dangerous journey, overcoming all obstacles he encounters along the way.[53] In this deeply allegorical work Uhlman fully explores his narrative skills, and succeeds in depicting and questioning the horrors of war.

In another untitled drawing (*Untitled*, Child with balloon among ruined buildings, Figure 13), the girl continues her journey through a world in ruins. She walks past destroyed buildings, dead bodies scattered in the street. To her left, a body hangs from a dead branch which is enmeshed in barbed wire (like all the trees depicted in Uhlman's other internment drawings, not included here). Is it Uhlman's intention to suggest that the tree of life has been suffocated? In her groundbreaking study on the influence of the Holocaust on the visual arts, Ziva Amishai-Maisels identifies the image of the thorned tree as a major symbol that stands for the torturing of humanity.[54] The crown of thorns has held an important place in the Western art tradition and in Christian iconography as a representation of Christ's suffering; thus the body hanging from the tree here could be seen as a representation of the body of Christ.

The moon breaks through the thick dark sky, the place being completely deserted but for the little girl in her white dress holding her balloon. Using conté and wash, Uhlman creates a halo effect around the girl and her dress, rendering her illuminated. Again, the inward intention of this work is to show the girl's strength and her resilience in carrying on with her march. The ruins lurk like monsters in the darkness. The building to the girl's right (possibly a destroyed church) appears to have a monster's face which looks as if it may attempt to devour the girl at any point. A poem, written in internment and dedicated 'for my child', describes Uhlman's fears and his hope of a better future for her. He predicts that his child, born during wartime, will experience years of suffering and hardship. He does, however, end the poem on a more hopeful note, predicting that happier times will follow.[55]

CHRISTIAN ICONOGRAPHY

In some of his internment work, as already seen, Uhlman draws on Christian iconography and biblical symbols (the crucified Christ, the Madonna and Child, the cross) to examine symbolically the theme of universal suffering.

In *Depiction and Interpretation*, Amishai-Maisels discusses the primary Holocaust symbols of the barbed wire, the child alone, memento mori, as well as biblical imagery (hope and redemption, mourning and silence) and the crucified Jew (Christ and the Church). It is remarkable that these are all themes Uhlman also used in his internment art works. Maisels observes that many of the symbols used by affected artists had artistic precedents, illustrating this with numerous examples. Similarly, it would seem likely that Uhlman who, as stated earlier, worked mainly from memory, used visual references that were already known to him, or were embedded in his personal and cultural German heritage; his knowledge of both Christian and Jewish iconography; or came from experiences gained during his time in Franco's Spain and pre-war Paris.

In his Internment Diary he notes that early childhood memories had made a big impact on him, and that in adult life he was 'governed by powerful childhood impressions'.[56] In *The Making of an Englishman,* Uhlman discusses these memories and his childhood and school experiences in great detail. He recalls several childhood incidents which had imprinted themselves on his memory and shaped both his sense of self and his lifelong ambivalence towards religion and his own Jewish background from an early age on. Born into a bourgeois German-Jewish family in Stuttgart, neither Uhlman's father nor mother were practising Jews. In fact, his father had chosen a Christian religious education for his son, thereby inadvertently being responsible for Uhlman's brief adherence to anti-Semitic views stemming from the religious education he received there – Uhlman's teacher of religious education 'talked about the Crucifixion with so much passion that he made quite a little anti-Semite out of me'.[57] Uhlman also recalls an incident at school when he was challenged by another Jewish boy about being Jewish himself. He remembers pushing the boy against a wall while retorting that he had had 'nothing to do with the murderers of Christ'.[58] At the age of nine Uhlman changed schools; from then on, he and the two other Jewish boys at the school were instructed by a rabbi. Uhlman remembered this period as one in which he 'was dumped into the lukewarm water of the rabbi's mild approach to Judaism';[59] and also recalled that 'there was little or no anti-Semitism' at the school.[60] By the age of seventeen Uhlman had become an atheist, finding it impossible to believe in the existence of a God who could tolerate all the human suffering around him. 'From now on I would have to live alone without any divine help or consolation.'[61]

However, Uhlman, like many other exiled artists, experienced a rapprochement with his own Jewish origins that was brought about by his later unsettling experience of anti-Semitism. Stripped of his German heritage when he was branded a Jew, he was compelled to leave his home country. Uhlman began, in internment, to display solidarity with other Jewish internees, and to develop an interest in and sympathy for his own Jewish cultural heritage, and the suffering endured by Jews. Although he remained an atheist throughout his life, he never denied or sought to hide his own Jewishness.

In her study, Amishai-Maisels demonstrates that one of the primary biblical symbols of the Holocaust victim was 'the crucified Jew, an image that was developed by Christians and Jews alike before the war to express Jewish persecution and martyrdom'.[62] However, in one of Uhlman's untitled internment drawings dedicated to his newborn child (*Untitled*, War fantasy with crucified Christ, Figure 14), Christ's relationship to the world is depicted in an entirely different way to that in Christian representations of the Crucifixion. In Christian depictions, Christ, the saviour of humanity, carries the world's suffering. In Uhlman's drawing, Christ's suffering is shared with humanity. His crucified Christ is surrounded by a world in ruins, dead bodies scattered everywhere. The little girl, present again in this scene, is shown without her balloon, her face turned away from the horrors surrounding her. This drawing does not concentrate all suffering within Christ; rather it depicts a more universal kind of suffering. Whereas in Christian religious symbolism the cross is often seen as a symbol of victory over death, portraying the intersection of a heavenly and eternal with a limited and earthly presence, here the crucified Christ is caught up in a world without redemption, where human suffering will prevail.

Thematically this drawing resembles Marc Chagall's iconoclastic painting *The White Crucifixion* (1938, oil on canvas), in which Christ is also caught in a world of despair. Although Christ is the central figure here, human suffering surrounds him; people are fleeing from burning homes. Franz Meyer, Chagall's biographer, comments: 'Though all the suffering of the world is mirrored in the Crucifixion, suffering remains man's lasting fate and is not abolished by Christ's death.'[63]

In Uhlman's drawing, discussed above, the little girl has again become a silent witness to the world's atrocities. This drawing, and others from the series, bear a resemblance to Goya's series 'The Disasters of War' (1810–14) which is not accidental. Goya, who was concerned with the theme of man's inhumanity to man and who had directly experienced and condemned the atrocities of war, in fact provided great inspiration for Uhlman. His diary entry on 6 October 1940 records his affinity to Goya: 'One does not have to add anything to a face, one must let it express itself, as it is. Goya did that. He didn't add, he reproduced and accepted what nature gave.' In Uhlman's work there are also visual references to Hieronymus Bosch and his visions of weird and hellish creatures, representing human choices and weaknesses.[64]

An untitled drawing (*Untitled*, Child hanging from a gallows, Figure 15) of one little girl hanging from an imposing gallows and a second girl with a balloon standing next to her is by far the most disturbing, the bleakest work of all. Here, the girl with the balloon stands frozen, turned from the viewer's gaze; in fact, the dead girl looks very similar to her. Two vultures and a barely visible quarter moon loom in the dark night sky.[65]

Both the dead and the living child are enveloped in darkness, the only other living creatures being the vultures, birds of death. This image differs from other drawings in that here the living girl seems helpless and lost in the dark, unable to rescue her dead counterpart. If we revisit Figure 12 (*Untitled*, Girl with balloon and gallows), a linocut discussed earlier, we recognize the same motif of the little girl standing helplessly next to a second female body hanging lifeless from a gallows.

Uhlman only used a limited number of visual referents, which he would revisit over and over again. This is the case with another untitled linocut *(Untitled,* Skull, flowers, gallows, Figure 16) that constitutes a direct reworking of an earlier Uhlman drawing of a human skull with flower and skeleton (this drawing became the frontispiece for *Captivity*). Here, Uhlman continues to be a prophet of disaster: a powerful memento mori, a large human skull with a dead flower between its teeth, dominates the image, to its right a gallows and a hanged man; a full moon, barbed wire, vultures and dead branches make up the background. On top of one of the dead branches there sits a lone songbird.

In his Internment Memoir, Uhlman recalls his feelings of ephemerality: 'I, like everyone else before me and after me, will disappear without leaving a trace.'[66] His realization of his own mortality is reflected in this and most other linocut prints. Towards the end of his life, this fear of not having made any significant impact grew even stronger, with the 1979 memoir containing many more references to death than the 1940 diary.

THE SHIP METAPHOR

Uhlman draws on a further memento mori as exemplified in his use of the ship metaphor. In a series of five drawings Uhlman worked with the visual referents of shipwrecks. His captivity on the Isle of Man within constant sight of the sea, coupled with serious depression, must at least in part have inspired this set of images. In *Das Totenschiff – The Ship of the Dead* (Figure 17) an emaciated man sits upright in a rowing boat. He has released his hold on the rudder and stares into the dark night. A corpse floats on its back, the dark sea beneath him, while the moon tries to break through the darkness. Another tall wave, and the rower may be swept into the sea as well.

A linocut, (*Untitled*, Boat and rowers, Figure 18) works with the same motif, though this time the tone of the work is somewhat more hopeful. Two men are depicted in a boat in rough sea; one of them, the rower, holds on tightly to the rudder, navigating the boat forward. A second faceless man, who may be dead, lies on his back. In the distance there is a second boat with a high sail, also containing two people. Although waves are crashing over the boats, there are seagulls in the sky, and the boats appear to be moving. The tone of the linocut is very different to that of the drawing, *The Ship of the Dead*, in which the man sits frozen, his face staring into the void; the entire drawing appears static. The linocut on the other hand appears more active; here the rower is apparently in control of his boat, moving with the strong wind. Moreover, he is not out at sea alone, there are other boats around him. Thus the linocut scene is more optimistic, the marks dynamic, and there is a strong sense of forward movement.

THE THEMES OF DEATH AND HOPE

The themes of death and hope are omnipresent in the drawings, linocuts and diary entries Uhlman created during internment. But their significance remains ambiguous: as the above examples have indicated, Uhlman's mood generally moves between sadness and despair. Yet at the same time, he also retains a hope for a new world after his release from the camp. Death and danger caused by National Socialism and war become challenges that are surmountable. Characteristic of this more optimistic view are the following two drawings.

In Figure 19 (*Untitled,* Dance of Death), the girl smiles in the face of death, is unafraid of it, and even seduces death into dancing with her. In Uhlman's interpretation of the dance of death theme (and in contrast to Hans Holbein the Younger's 1525 woodcut series of the same name), life triumphs over death. Uhlman continued with this more hopeful theme in several more drawings, for instance in *Little Girl with War Criminals* (Figure 20). In a letter written to Raymond Mortimer, from which the latter quoted in his introduction to *Captivity*, Uhlman explained that he had been pondering over the question of 'responsibility for all the misery and horror of our time; and out of the dark marched a long line of war-criminals, the sinister shapes of false priests […] capitalists, kings, dictators, fanatics'.[67] Holding her balloon, and only a fraction of their size, the girl looks up at the four war criminals with curiosity. While she appears healthy, the war criminals are portrayed as skeletons still clutching their symbols of power, the dictator adorned with his medals, a helmet, sabre and sword. The king wears his crown, the priest bears a cross, and the fourth (possibly a judge) is dressed in what could be a judge's robe. This drawing alludes to the ephemeral nature of power, contrasting greed and corruption with innocence and honesty.

'ECCLESIA MILITANS' SERIES

A further set of images to emerge during this time, the 'Ecclesia Militans' series, examined the role of the Church, particularly as a handmaiden to fascism in Spain leading up to and during the Spanish Civil War, and its role in Nazi Germany as a handmaiden to anti-Semitism. Here, the symbols of death are projected onto the political enemy – in this case the Catholic Church as a servant to fascism – and are indicative of an inhumane and dangerous world which has been condemned to perish. The final two images, which will be discussed only briefly, are from this series which totals more than thirty drawings inspired by experiences in Spain in 1936. They all appear to have been completed between July and September 1940.[68]

While staying in Tossa del Mar in 1936, Uhlman had witnessed the looting of the local church by a group of Spanish anarchists. He describes this incident and other acts of opposition to the church in *The Making of an Englishman*.[69] In 'Ecclesia Militans', he works with his knowledge of the role of the Spanish Catholic Church in supporting and conspiring with Franco and his brutal fascist regime, putting the church and Spanish priests under scrutiny. He later explained that the series was a 'bitter and savage attack, not against religion, but against the Church, particularly in Spain which betrayed Christ'.[70] 'Corrupted by wealth and power',[71] the Catholic priests depicted in an untitled drawing from the 'Ecclesia Militans' series (Figure 21) have exchanged their crosses for swastikas. The priest foregrounded in the drawing also wears the Star of David around his neck. Like bats or vultures, the priests fly over burning villages wearing satisfied expressions on their haunting faces.

It is clear that Uhlman also intended a critique of the Church in Nazi Germany, where religious leaders and church officials nurtured anti-Semitism. A 1934 photomontage by John Heartfield portrays a row of hooded priests, bearing crosses that have turned into large swastikas. The caption below reads: 'Hey, [you] over there, move the cross further to the right.'[72] This photomontage and Uhlman's drawings both recognize the role that the Church, as an institution, played in supporting the Hitler regime.

In the final drawing reproduced in this volume, *Clothing Caught on a Branch and Lying in a Field* (Figure 22), the garments worn by the priests in other drawings reappear. The two scarecrows look like disembodied priests, and were probably drawn after Uhlman had completed the 'Ecclesia Militans' series. On 2 October 1940, at a time when he himself felt agitated, he noted in his Internment Diary that he had made a drawing of windswept scarecrows. The garment caught on the branch looks as if it has been pierced through and through while skeletal fingers 'grow' from the sleeves. The deflated, disembodied garments are cast adrift in a desolate, nondescript and windswept landscape with Uhlman's trademark vultures present in the background. Both a political commentary on an unanchored world cast adrift, and possibly a personal expression of Uhlman's own sense of a life cast adrift, this drawing again typifies much of the art work produced by him during this difficult period.

* * * * *

With fewer than twenty drawings and linocuts considered here out of more than 150 produced during internment, a number of questions remain. Most importantly, perhaps, it seems appropriate to ask why Uhlman's artworks deserve any particular attention now. For many years his small collection of linocuts has lain virtually forgotten in a folder at the Documents Department at the Imperial War Museum. Uhlman's drawings held in the IWM Arts Department and elsewhere have hardly seen the light of day. None of the institutions or museums to which Uhlman donated his works have ever staged a major (or even minor) retrospective of his art works and very few art historians or other scholars have devoted time to them. One exception is Anna Müller-Härlin who in her doctoral thesis concludes that the significance of Uhlman's internment work does not lie in the fact that they are groundbreaking art works but rather that their importance lies in the themes he explored.

Therefore, in the present chapter, an attempt has been made to consider Uhlman's art works within the context of their production. It can be argued that Uhlman was trapped both physically and artistically: as an exiled person in captivity, with a limited artistic palette, he was in a precarious position and to some extent became an outsider.

It is true that because of his naïve style and lack of formal training, critics have tended to view his work as simplistic. Indeed, Klaus Hinrichsen has commented on Uhlman's 'limited atmosphere and its limited range', characterizing him as a 'natural primitive painter'. He does, however, describe Uhlman's pictures as possessing feeling and atmosphere, and considers his work 'genuine'. Uhlman's pictures, so Hinrichsen has claimed, 'in some way also conveyed the sense of the times'.[73]

It can, then, be argued that Uhlman's art works have both testimonial and artistic value and that Uhlman succeeded in documenting his own entrapment and that of fellow internees. Although the internal structure of each of his drawings is simple, Uhlman's personal iconography is universally understandable and many of his drawings show compassion. All his internment drawings and linocut prints are devoid of colour, being rendered in stark black and white lines. While some of the works discussed in this chapter are of a very descriptive nature and scarcely move beneath the surface of the material, others have far greater visual strength.[74]

It has already been established that, shortly after being interned, Uhlman stopped painting entirely; instead, he preferred the immediacy of drawing. Thus drawing became extremely important to him, not as a way to draft a sketch for a painting but as a means of expression in its own right. Elsewhere, art critic John Berger has argued that, while the practice of drawing is relatively simple compared to painting, its fundamental distinction is 'in the working of the artist's mind'.[75] He explains the enormous potential of drawing over any other form of mark making as follows: 'Drawing is a way of learning to leave the present or rather of gathering the future, the present and the past into one.'[76] Uhlman was certainly attracted to drawing as it mirrored the rawness and unpredictability of his own experience and the lack of structure in his life. In his technically more astute drawings, experiences from different areas of his life (his own past, his captivity, the unknown future, inner turmoil) collapse into one timeless scenario. When Berger discusses the power of art and drawing, he could be referring to one of Uhlman's dark internment drawings: 'Everything that has been and will be is somewhere instantaneously there if one can only be open to it.'[77]

It was Klaus Hinrichsen who provided a second pressing reason to re-examine Uhlman's work in reminding us that much of internment art would have been labelled degenerate in Germany and its production would have been severely punished: 'German Art, strangled by cultural barbarians at home, survived in British internment camps.'[78]

More recently, Jutta Vinzent has considered 'the extent to which the prevailing circumstances led to the development of a particular aesthetic'.[79] However, no distinct, internment aesthetic emerges from her analysis. In her exhaustive study *Zeichnen im Exil – Zeichen des Exils*, Rosamunde Neugebauer suggests instead that aesthetic symbols can be found in the works of exiled artists which can be read, or viewed, as expressions and circumstantial evidence of their experience of exile. She concludes that, far from having been avant-garde or innovative in style, drawings produced in exile drew heavily on traditional motifs, often returning to, and revisiting themes borrowed from older traditions within painting.[80] However, she argues that for people like Fred Uhlman the newness consisted in making the artwork in the first place. Without ever receiving any artistic training, he embraced the artistic process in order to reinvent himself as an artist.[81]

The overarching strand that connected much of the artistic production of the internees appears to have been that they engaged in artistic processes in proactive and resourceful ways, making creative use of existing materials and adapting their art practice to fit available resources. Vinzent adds further that the 'expression of inner needs was not a means of escape from [the artists'] situation, but a way of dealing with it. Putting their fears and feelings on a piece of paper, a linocut or on a canvas relieved the internees' distress. The process of producing art was in itself a form of therapy'.[82]

The cathartic nature of art production during internment in order to work through fears can be seen as a form of resistance and an attempt, by Uhlman, to consolidate his sense of personal identity. In both his 1940 Diary and the 1979 Internment Memoir, Uhlman draws the conclusion that the production of art was a survival mechanism. This is a point made by Yvonne Cresswell, also, who discusses internment art as a form of escape in her exhibition catalogue *Living with the Wire: Civilian Internment in the Isle of Man during the two World Wars*.[83]

In conclusion, one should not judge Uhlman's internment works on their artistic quality and merit alone, but on their capacity to mediate experience and provide testimony. An interned artist-witness, Uhlman succeeded in conveying a widely experienced trauma and, as an artist, attempted to 'describe' and comment on one of the most tragic periods of the twentieth century. His images may be naïve, but in their rawness they do not aestheticize universal suffering but instead portray it in compassionate ways.

NOTES

1. Uhlman, Internment Diary, 23 September 1940.
2. From an article on Uhlman by Nigel Reynolds, *Hampstead and Highgate Express*, 30 May 1980, p.47, Imperial War Museum [IWM] Art Department, Fred Uhlman folder.
3. The exact number of art works produced is difficult to establish as indicated in the Introduction to this volume. In a postscript to his 1979 Internment Memoir Uhlman talks of 200 drawings; elsewhere the number fluctuates between 100 and 150. Uhlman also produced a small number of oil paintings and experimented with sculpture and lithographs which do not appear to have survived. While twenty-four drawings were published in *Captivity* in 1946, the vast majority of surviving art works (including eleven linocuts, held in the Department of Documents, IWM) have not been published before. Almost all illustrations mentioned in this chapter are reproduced in the present volume (see List of Illustrations).
4. 'I have started on a small sculpture and have written six poems that I have illustrated for you with linocuts', Uhlman letter to Diana, 12 November 1940. An example of such a poem and linocut combination has been reproduced in this volume as Figure 23.
5. Walter Zander, 'The power of the spirit in internment', *Adventures in Reconciliation*, IFOR Leaflet No. 7, 1941, IWM, Art Department, Fred Uhlman folder.
6. E.g. Klaus Hinrichsen, 'Visual Arts behind the Wire', in David Cesarani and Tony Kushner (eds), *The Internment of Aliens in Twentieth-Century Britain* (London: Frank Cass, 1993), pp.188–209; and Paul Jacobsthal, 'The Long Vac 1940', in R.M. Cooper (ed.), *Refugee Scholars: Conversations with Tess Simpson* (Leeds: Morland Books, 1992), pp.208–28.
7. Michael Seyfert, *Im Niemandsland: Deutsche Exilliteratur in britischer Internierung: Ein unbekanntes Kapitel der Kulturgeschichte des Zweiten Weltkriegs* (Berlin: Das Arsenal, 1984).
8. See, for example, Monica Bohm-Duchen and Zuleika Dobson (eds), *Art in Exile in Great Britain 1933–1945* (London: Camden Arts Centre, 1986); Yvonne Cresswell (ed.), *Living with the Wire: Civilian Internment in the Isle of Man during the two World Wars* (Douglas: Manx National Heritage, 1994); Jessica Feather, *Art Behind Barbed Wire* (Liverpool: National Museums, 2004).
9. Jutta Vinzent, 'Aesthetics of Internment Art in Britain during the Second World War', pp.81–92, in Helga Schreckenberger (ed.), *Aesthetiken des Exils* (Amsterdam: Rodopi, 2003); Rosamunde Neugebauer, *Zeichnen im Exil – Zeichen des Exils? Handzeichnung und Druckgraphik deutschsprachiger Emigranten ab 1933* (Weimar: VDG, 2003).
10. Fred Uhlman, *The Making of an Englishman* (London: Gollancz, 1960), p.312.
11. Anna Müller-Härlin (formerly Plodeck), 'The Making of Fred Uhlman: Life and Work of the Painter and Writer in Exile' (unpublished doctoral thesis, Courtauld Institute of Art, University of London, 2004), pp.122–47. See also Anna Müller-Härlin, 'Fred Uhlman's Internment Drawings', in Shulamith Behr and Marian Malet (eds), *Arts in Exile in Britain 1933–1945: Politics and Cultural Identity: Yearbook of the Research Centre for German and Austrian Exile Studies*, 6 (2004), pp.135–63.
12. Hinrichsen, 'Visual Arts behind the Wire', p.198.
13. Internment Diary, 29 September 1940.
14. Jacobsthal, 'The Long Vac 1940', p.223.
15. In fact he must have been thinking about them. Earlier, he had obtained a travel document and ticket for his sister Erna but she had decided not to leave Germany without her furniture. By the time he was interned and had received a final telegram it was too late: 'There was nothing I could do. It was definitely and forever too late. My information is that towards the end of 1944 Erna threw herself under a train with her baby on the way to Auschwitz' (*The Making of an Englishman*, p.32). Uhlman's parents both died in Theresienstadt in 1943.
16. Jacobsthal, 'The Long Vac 1940', p.223.
17. Jacobsthal commented that he had not suffered in internment to the degree that others had: 'Uhlman's vision of death, barbed wire and crucifixion, admirable as they were, expressed a feeling strange to me' ('The Long Vac 1940', p.223).
18. Hinrichsen, ' Visual Arts behind the Wire', pp.68–9.
19. Internment Diary, 23 September 1940.
20. Hinrichsen, 'Visual Arts behind the Wire', p.197.

21. Monica Bohm-Duchen, in Foreword to *Art in Exile in Great Britain 1933–1945*.
22. Ibid.
23. Internment Diary, 14 September 1940.
24. He documented this in the self-portrait: 'My bedroom – the artist uses his suitcase as a work surface in the absence of a table', 1940 (IWM AS LD7532), ink, wash, conté on paper, 177 mm x 228 mm.
25. Although there are several slightly different accounts as to how he obtained ink and charcoal, in each case Uhlman clearly states that Diana had given them to him: in his 1979 Memoir, Uhlman writes that Diana 'had put some Indian ink, charcoal, a pen and a block of writing paper in my suitcase' (26 June 1940). In *The Making of an Englishman* he describes how on 25 June Diana had brought some paper, ink and a fountain pen to the police station where he was being held, commenting that: 'It was the most marvellous present, she could have thought of nothing more useful for keeping up my morale' (p.225). In addition, the AIA and other organizations supplied art materials to the camp, and there were local art suppliers on the island, too (Hinrichsen, 'Visual Arts Behind the Wire', p.194).
26. See Internment Memoir, 15 September 1940: 'Particularly brushes, paper, ink.'
27. In his 1940 Internment Diary he records completing three oil paintings by 3 September. These may have been the same paintings, *Douglas, Ascot, View of Douglas*, as are mentioned in the catalogue to the Second Art Exhibition that opened on 19 November 1940. Unfortunately the present location of these paintings is unknown.
28. Internment Memoir, 19 October 1940.
29. I am grateful to Caroline Compton and Anna Müller-Härlin for pointing this out to me. Hinrichsen also records that during internment Erich Kahn is believed to have invented a printing technique on wax stencils which made the print look like a lithograph ('Visual Arts Behind the Wire', p.195).
30. Hinrichsen, 'Visual Arts Behind the Wire', p.195.
31. Internment Diary, 10 November 1940.
32. Ibid., 18 November 1940.
33. Internment Memoir, 11 November 1940.
34. Ibid., 18 December 1940.
35. Müller-Härlin, 'Fred Uhlman's Internment Drawings', p.138.
36. Unfortunately Uhlman himself did not go into any detail about the content, symbolism, sequencing or the reasons behind the themes of his artistic output in either his 1940 Diary or his 1979 Memoir.
37. The 'Ecclesia Militans' series is covered in greater detail by Müller-Härlin in 'The Making of Fred Uhlman', pp.141–4.
38. Internment Memoir, 25 June 1940.
39. Internment Diary, 25 June 1940.
40. 'I know it's nothing special. Nothing that hasn't occurred a thousand times before and yet the sensitive person will continue to experience it as torture, horror, humiliation,' Internment Diary, 25 June 1940. Another, perhaps unconscious reason for the faces drawn using minimal markers may have been Uhlman's interest in African masks, which had begun in the early 1930s. African masks frequently only have lines for eyes and a cut indicating the mouth, reflecting their archetypical quality (and are in this way indeed similar to the faces Uhlman drew in internment).
41. Internment Memoir, section entitled 'New Chapter', preceding entry of 7 September 1940.
42. Seyfert, *Im Niemandsland*, p.74.
43. Interview with Klaus Hinrichsen, 'Civilian Internment in Britain 1939–1945', IWM, Department of Sound Records, 003789.
44. Ibid., p.66.
45. Hinrichsen, 'Visual Arts Behind the Wire', p.204.
46. Seyfert, *Im Niemandsland*, p.74.
47. The figure of the girl with the balloon appears to have emerged on 19 October, when Uhlman first mentions her in his Internment Diary. There he writes that he has made a drawing of a child and gallows and feels deeply depressed. 'Everything looks black. Will I ever get out? How much longer?'

48. Internment Memoir, final section entitled 'The Drawings'.
49. Ibid.
50. Müller-Härlin, 'Fred Uhlman's Internment Drawings', p.145.
51. Nigel Reynolds, *Hampstead and Highgate Express*, 30 May 1980, p.47.
52. See 'Faschistische Ruhmesmale', 22 April 1936, in Wieland Herzfelde, *John Heartfield* (Dresden: Verlag der Kunst, 1986), p.175.
53. In fact Uhlman attended Günther Zuntz's lectures on Odysseus while in Hutchinson Camp. Rosamunde Neugebauer devotes an entire section to the influence and significance of the story of the Odyssey on drawings produced in exile in her *Zeichnen im Exil – Zeichen des Exils* (see 'Der "vielgewanderte" Heimkehrer Odysseus und die Suche eines Esels nach seiner Heimat', pp.267–75).
54. Ziva Amishai-Maisels, *Depiction and Interpretation: The Influence of the Holocaust on the Visual Arts* (Oxford/New York: Pergamon, 1993), p.133.
55. IWM Documents folder, 78/19/1.
56. Cf. Internment Diary, 5 November 1940.
57. Uhlman, *The Making of an Englishman*, p.33.
58. Ibid.
59. Ibid., p.37.
60. Ibid., pp.35–6.
61. Ibid., p.51.
62. Amishai-Maisels, *Depiction and Interpretation*, p.155. Prior to the Holocaust there had, of course, already been a long tradition amongst Jewish artists in making use of biblical imagery which provided them with well known and universally understood symbols that could be used to symbolize contemporary experiences.
63. Franz Meyer, *Marc Chagall: Life and Work* (New York: Abrams, 1964), p.414.
64. In 'The Making of Fred Uhlman', Müller-Härlin discusses marked references to Bosch in an analysis of the grotesque image (pp.140–1).
65. In light of the fact that over one and a half million children died in the Holocaust, this image takes on a much more haunting quality than Uhlman could have predicted in 1940. The image of the child alone or the unknown dead child was indeed a distinctive Holocaust symbol, as Amishai-Maisels details (*Depiction and Interpretation*, p.143).
66. 10/11/12 December 1940, recalled in Internment Memoir.
67. Raymond Mortimer, Introduction to *Captivity* (London: Jonathan Cape, 1946).
68. Cf. Internment Diary, 29 September 1940: 'probably the conclusion to the "ecclesia militans" cycle.' On the 'Ecclesia Militans' series, see Müller-Härlin, 'The Making of Fred Uhlman', pp.141–7. The series is held at the IWM.
69. Uhlman, *The Making of an Englishman*, pp.192–4.
70. 'The Drawings', in final section of Internment Memoir, 1979.
71. Raymond Mortimer in Introduction to *Captivity*.
72. Wieland Herzfelde, *John Heartfield*, p.143: 'Der Reichsbischof richtet das Christentum aus.'
73. Hinrichsen Interview, pp.70–1.
74. For the former, see for example most of the linocuts (at which Uhlman was a novice). An example of the latter would be the *Ship of the Dead*.
75. John Berger, *Permanent Red: Essays in Seeing* (London: Methuen, 1960), pp.183–4.
76. Berger, 'Night Waves', 28 March 2005, BBC Radio 3.
77. Ibid.
78. Hinrichsen, 'Visual Arts Behind the Wire', p.188.
79. Vinzent, 'Aesthetics of Internment Art', p.71.
80. 'Artists in exile neither developed a new, shared style nor did they expand the spectrum of techniques and media in any significant way' (Neugebauer, *Zeichnen im Exil – Zeichen des Exils*, p.313).
81. See ibid. who, quoting from Uhlman's autobiography, writes that while he regretted never becoming a great artist, the experience of exile brought him a little closer to this dream.
82. Vinzent, 'Aesthetics of Internment Art', p.83.
83. Cresswell (ed.), 'Living with the Wire', pp.53ff.

9. *Epilogue*

Anna Müller-Härlin

When Uhlman joined his wife and their daughter Caroline on 1 January 1941 in the countryside in Bambers Green, he wanted to forget the traumatic last half year as quickly as possible. For the next few years, before moving back to London for good, he led an uneventful life in the country where he was met with kindness by his neighbours and obeyed the travel restrictions for 'enemy aliens'. He joined the local fire-watchers, painted, grew vegetables and bred rabbits.[1] His son Francis was born there in 1943; Uhlman met up with neighbours like the painter Kenneth Rowntree, and sometimes visitors came from London, among them his newly made friends from internment such as the art historian Klaus Hinrichsen and his wife.[2]

Although he was geographically cut off from the London art scene, Uhlman continued to exhibit successfully in London throughout the war. This was exceptional, as at that time the English public generally paid very little attention to contemporary German art and exiled German-speaking artists. Other refugee artists such as Oskar Kokoschka, who had been famous on the continent, struggled for public attention in England. In 1942, Uhlman's second solo exhibition in London was arranged, held at the Leicester Galleries.[3] In Britain, throughout the 1940s, a preference for the figurative and a specific Romantic sentiment prevailed, culminating in Neo-Romanticism. While artists and critics generally propagated Neo-Romanticism as a quality deeply rooted in British art, however, Uhlman's work was seen as imbued with precisely such Romantic qualities.[4]

As already mentioned, some of his internment drawings were exhibited at the house of the Free German League of Culture in

1942, and in 1946 a selection of twenty-four of the drawings was published by Jonathan Cape, entitled *Captivity*. Uhlman always had a high estimation of his works from the internment episode. However, he considered this specific artistic output behind barbed wire as directly linked to his experience as an internee. After his release, none of Uhlman's paintings dealt with the issue of internment. Neither did he take up the powerful themes from his drawings and linocuts again, such as the girl and her balloon, the priests or the shipwrecks, in his works after 1940. It is true that some of the motifs that he employed while interned like the barbed wire fences or the skull with the flower reoccur, however these had already played a role in his pre-internment paintings. In the early 1940s, as in 1939, he often juxtaposed despairing war landscapes with a still life; a destroyed building demonstrated the destructive force of war. In addition, he now looked to the English countryside for inspiration, too. Often, these paintings featured cathedrals, or ruins of Gothic churches. The melancholy of Uhlman's paintings in these years bore a strong resemblance to the work of some of his British colleagues like John Piper, whose work expressed a Romantic backward-looking perspective.

Uhlman continued to be a well-respected painter in England into the 1950s. In the post-war years, the subjects of his paintings became more lighthearted: topics such as the Queen's Coronation festivities in 1953 stand in sharp contrast to the gloomy landscapes he had painted previously. A journey to New York in 1955 triggered his most ambitious series of paintings in terms of form. Indeed, an imaginary New York skyline became his primary motif for the next few years, his canvases now often reaching a height of almost a metre. They became a means for him to explore the possibilities of abstraction, the skyscrapers set against a plain background. In contrast to these unusual works, however, he also painted winter landscapes and paintings of cranes, which often ran the risk of being merely decorative.

With a younger generation of artists and a growing awareness of the international art scene, however, new experimental developments gained ascendancy in Britain. It was in the 1960s that the interest of the art scene in Uhlman's work waned and attention shifted from London to the provinces, where his work was regularly shown in small galleries in solo and group exhibitions (these exhibitions arousing little or no interest in London, however).[5] Indeed Uhlman grew to be increasingly perceived as a Welsh painter, his love for the Welsh landscape having originated during the war.[6] Uhlman's Welsh paintings have as their main characteristics slender, lifeless trees and a calm, peaceful sky often lit by a moon. In the 1970s, public interest in Uhlman's work diminished further and he sank into oblivion as an artist. The decline in his career had a lasting impact on his self-confidence and self-esteem; his growing depression finds strong expression in his late œuvre: the gloomy Welsh landscapes are now apocalyptic visions painted by Uhlman in the expectation of death.

The success of his novella *Reunion* in the late 1970s and early 1980s provided Uhlman with a substitute for the lack of public interest in his paintings in the last decades of his life. A further source of satisfaction for him was his collection of African sculpture, which he had begun in Paris in the 1930s. In 1983, he donated his collection, consisting of over seventy pieces, to the Hatton Gallery, Newcastle upon Tyne, where since 1984 it has been permanently on public display.

Fred Uhlman's life and work in exile were certainly exceptional. Having been a 'provincial lawyer in a provincial town', as he recalled in his autobiography in 1960,[7] the conditions of exile enabled him to change his profession, and to adopt a career as a painter, and later as a writer. The positive reception of Uhlman's work both in Paris and London at the beginning of his career was extraordinary. The intrepid courage he displayed in painting despite his lack of artistic training aroused interest in his work, and even today he still strikes us as an unusual painter. Uhlman was never able to keep up with modern experiments nor was he interested in them, but his work continuously developed, undergoing various changes over the decades. His œuvre is largely forgotten today, but he remains a rare example of a German-speaking refugee artist who, at least at one stage in his career, was included in the British art scene.

Uhlman regarded England as his new home, but one must also bear in mind that he never ceased to feel that he was a foreigner. His flight from Germany and his subsequent exile constituted a traumatic experience for him. Uhlman was haunted by the extermination of his family and the loss of his former home throughout his life as an 'Englishman'. Moreover, the difficulties of achieving acceptance within a society which continued to identify him as a foreigner, often merely because of his accent, should not be dismissed, while his experience of internment and his public exclusion as an 'enemy alien', though brief, added to his feelings of bitterness. The series of internment drawings, the linocuts and poetry from his time on the Isle of Man testify to his sensitive and often depressed state of mind. Nevertheless, he never gave up his attempt to assimilate, even if this proved only partly successful. It is striking, however, that in his mid-seventies he should choose to return once again to his experience of life as an 'enemy alien' and to translate and recast his original internment diary, apparently driven by an urge to bear testimony to his captivity to future generations.

NOTES

1. Fred Uhlman, *The Making of an Englishman* (London: Gollancz, 1960), p.244.
2. Letter from Klaus Hinrichsen to the author, 18 July 2003. The painter and art dealer E.L.T. Mesens also visited the Uhlmans in Essex during the war, as Uhlman recalled in 'Journal of a Painter', I (1965–70), British Library, ADD 74735, p.210.
3. 'Exhibition of Recent Paintings by Fred Uhlman', Leicester Galleries, London, 8–31 December 1942.
4. Raymond Mortimer, 'Preface', in ibid.
5. For example 'Fred Uhlman: 25 Years in Retrospect', Powys Hall, Bangor, 12–19 March 1960; 'Paintings by Fred Uhlman', Howard Roberts Gallery, Cardiff, 26 April–14 May 1960.
6. The Uhlmans went on holiday to Wales from the mid-1940s onwards. From the early 1950s, they had a house near Llanfrothen.
7. Uhlman, *The Making of An Englishman*, p.136.

Select Bibliography

Borchard, Ruth, *The Service Exchange in an Internment Camp* (London: Friends' Book Centre, 1943).

Brinson, Charmian, '"In the exile of internment" or "Von Versuchen aus einer Not eine Tugend zu machen": German-speaking women interned by the British during the Second World War', in William Niven and James Jordan (eds), *Politics and Culture in Twentieth-Century Germany* (Rochester, NY: Camden House, 2003), pp.63–87.

Brinson, Charmian, '"Keine verlorene Zeit": Musik im britischen Internierungslager Rushen', in Anne-Christine Rhode-Juechtern and Maria Kublitz-Kramer (eds), *Echolos: Klangwelten verfolgter Musikerinnen in der NS-Zeit* (Bielefeld: Aesthesis Verlag, 2003), pp.243–64.

Brinson, Charmian, 'The Anglican Bishop, the Methodist Minister and the Women of Rushen: George Bell, J. Benson Harrison and their Work for Women Internees', in *Humanitas*, 7, 2 (April 2006), pp.111–28.

Cesarani, David, and Kushner, Tony, *The Internment of Aliens in Twentieth-Century Britain* (London: Frank Cass, 1993).

Chappel, Connery, *Island of Barbed Wire* (London: Robert Hale, 1984).

Clarke, Alan, 'Theatre Behind Barbed Wire: German Refugee Theatre in British Internment', in Günter Berghaus (ed.), *Theatre and Film in Exile: German Artists in Britain, 1933–1945* (Oxford/New York/ Munich: Berg, 1989), pp.189–222.

Cresswell, Yvonne (ed.), *Living with the Wire: Civilian Internment in the Isle of Man during the two World Wars* (Douglas: Manx National Heritage, 1994).

Dove, Richard, 'KZ auf Englisch: Robert Neumann's Internment Diary', in Charmian Brinson, Richard Dove, Marian Malet, Jennifer Taylor (eds), *'England? Aber wo liegt es?' Deutsche und österreichische Emigranten in Grossbritannien, 1933–1945* (Munich: iudicium, 1996, pp.157–67).

Dove, Richard (ed.), *'Totally Un-English?': Britain's Internment of*

'Enemy Aliens' in Two World Wars: Yearbook of the Research Centre for German and Austrian Exile Studies, 7 (2005).

Feather, Jessica, *Art behind Barbed Wire* (Liverpool: National Museums Liverpool, 2004).

Gál, Hans, *Musik hinter Stacheldraht: Tagebuchblätter aus dem Sommer 1940* (Berne/ Berlin/Brussels/Frankfurt: Lang, 2003).

Gillman, Leni and Peter, *'Collar the Lot!' How Britain Expelled and Interned its Wartime Refugees* (London/Melbourne/New York: Quartet, 1980).

Kahn, Leo, *Obliging Fellow* (London: Nicholson and Watson, 1946).

Kapp, Yvonne and Mynatt, Margaret, *British Policy and the Refugees 1933–1941* (London: Frank Cass, 1997).

Kochan, Miriam, *Britain's Internees in the Second World War* (London: Macmillan, 1980).

Koenen, Emmy, 'Exil in England: Leben und Kampf im Frauenlager', in *Beiträge zur Geschichte der Arbeiterbewegung*, 20 (1978), pp.880–95.

Kunst im Exil in Grossbritannien 1933–1945 (exhibition catalogue of the Neue Gesellschaft für Bildende Kunst, 1983) (Berlin: Frölich and Kaufmann, 1986).

Lafitte, François, *The Internment of Aliens* (Harmondsworth: Penguin, 1940) (republished in 1988 by Libris, London).

Laurent, Livia, *A Tale of Internment* (London: George Allen and Unwin, 1942).

Lomnitz, Alfred, *'Never Mind Mr Lom!' or The Uses of Adversity* (London: Macmillan, 1941).

Müller-Härlin, Anna, 'Fred Uhlman's Internment Drawings', in Shulamith Behr and Marian Malet (eds), *Arts in Exile in Britain 1933–1945: Politics and Cultural Identity: Yearbook of the Research Centre for German and Austrian Exile Studies*, 6 (2004), pp.135–63.

Nelki, Erna, 'Eingesperrt im englischen Frauenlager', in Walter Zadek (ed.), *Sie flohen vor dem Hakenkreuz: Selbstzeugnisse der Emigranten: Ein Lesebuch für Deutsche* (Hamburg: Rowohlt, 1981), pp.120-6.

Nelki, Erna, 'Im englischen Frauenlager auf der Insel Man', in Gisela Dischner (ed.), *Eine stumme Generation berichtet: Frauen der dreissiger und vierziger Jahre* (Frankfurt: Fischer, 1982), pp.63–9.

Pearl, Cyril, *The Dunera Scandal* (London/Sydney/Melbourne: Angus and Robertson, 1983).

Seller, Maxine Schwartz, *We Built Up Our Lives: Education and Community among Jewish Refugees Interned by Britain in World War II* (Westport, CT: Greenwood Press, 2001).

Seyfert, Michael, *Im Niemandsland: Deutsche Exilliteratur in britischer Internierung: Ein unbekanntes Kapitel der Kulturgeschichte des Zweiten Weltkriegs* (Berlin: Das Arsenal, 1984).

Seyfert, Michael, 'His Majesty's Most Loyal Internees' in Gerhard Hirschfeld (ed.), *Exile in Great Britain: Refugees from Hitler's Germany* (Leamington Spa: Berg, 1984).

Stent, Ronald, *A Bespattered Page? The Internment of His Majesty's 'Most Loyal Enemy Aliens'* (London: André Deutsch, 1980).

Uhlman, Fred, *Captivity* (London: Jonathan Cape, 1946).

Uhlman, Fred, *The Making of an Englishman* (London: Gollancz, 1960).

Index